Unleash
Your
Dreams

UNLEASH
YOUR
DREAMS

Tame Your Hidden Fears
and Live the Life You Were Meant to Live

MICHAEL E. SILVERMAN, PH.D.

WILEY

John Wiley & Sons, Inc.

Published by John Wiley & Sons, Inc., Hoboken, New Jersey
Published simultaneously in Canada

Design and composition by Navta Associates, Inc.

For general information about our other products and services, please contact our Customer Care Department within the United States at (800) 762-2974, outside the United States at (317) 572-3993 or fax (317) 572-4002.

Wiley also publishes its books in a variety of electronic formats. Some content that appears in print may not be available in electronic books. For more information about Wiley products, visit our web site at www.wiley.com.

Library of Congress Cataloging-in-Publication Data:
Silverman, Michael, date.
  Unleash your dreams : tame your hidden fears and live the life you were
meant to live / Michael Silverman.
      p. cm.
  Includes bibliographical references (p.) and index.
  ISBN 978-0-470-13714-7 (cloth)
1. Fear. 2. Success. I. Title.
  BF575.F2S48 2008
  152.4'6—dc22

                                                                      2008001361

Printed in the United States of America

10 9 8 7 6 5 4 3 2 1

To my father

Prior to the completion of this manuscript, my father's illness took a turn for the worse. One day as we sat in his hospital room in Boston, we had an unusual conversation, one that I had yearned for my entire life, yet, as it unfolded, also regarded with dread.

My father was a quiet and uniquely private person. We rarely had conversations of a personal nature. Rather, we tended to speak about things like the local sports teams, the right tool for a household job, or my professional development. If anything, our conversations seemed one-sided: I doing the talking, he doing the critiquing.

I remember as a kid I used to sneak through my father's dresser drawers just to try to get a glimpse of what made him tick. But baseballs, Zippo lighters, and a handful of old coins and medals never really amounted to much information. Then, after nearly forty years, part of my father that had been unknown to me was now accessible—and I found his words at times uncomfortable to hear.

As he spoke to me from his hospital bed, I learned about the joys and sorrows he felt at the completion of his life. I learned about the opportunities that he'd never taken advantage of and the regrets he had for not doing so. Most surprisingly, I learned how much my accomplishments had meant to him and how much joy they had brought him. At the end of our conversation, when I told him that I would be dedicating this book to him, his response was, as usual, self-deprecating: "Why?"

My father may never have fully understood how positive a force he was in my life, but after our conversation I had no doubts about how strong and good-natured he really was. Although he never got the chance to read these words, I dedicate this book to a loving father who gave me the permission to pursue my dreams—even if it meant that I would go on to accomplish some of his.

Contents

PART THREE

Decide What Matters Most

Acknowledgments

Writing a book while simultaneously maintaining an academic appointment, a clinical practice, and a neurobehavioral research program within a major metropolitan medical center is no easy task. I've frequently been told by those who care about me the most that I tend to take on way too much at once. Luckily, I have learned the importance of asking for a helping hand every once in a while—and I've been lucky enough to get some much-needed help in return.

No one has offered more help with the completion of this manuscript than Rachel Kranz. In truth, this book would never have been completed without her, her insight, and her ability at times to seemingly read my mind. On the same note, I need to thank Janis Vallely, my literary agent, not only for introducing me to Rachel, but also for believing in me and what I have to say. Thank you as well to Tom Miller at John Wiley & Sons for his initial and ongoing support of me as an author with something to offer, and to John Simko for his careful shepherding of the manuscript to completion.

Thank you to my colleagues at the Mount Sinai School of Medicine for their support, understanding, and flexibility. Particularly, I need to thank my colleague codirector, and friend Martin Goldstein, M.D., a truly gifted physician, educator, and patient advocate. Marty, your professional and personal philosophy truly exemplifies the best in individualized patient and family care—

bar none. Thank you to those in our Neurobehavioral Research Group, especially Leslie Delfiner, a brilliant student and soon to be a brilliant clinician; Michal Safier, who single-handedly managed one of our most important clinical research projects; and Mariel Gallego, who despite her own research obligations in the lab offered to pick up the ball when Michal needed to begin focusing on her doctoral dissertation. Thank you to Molly Morgan; although she hasn't been with us very long, she has brought with her a new perspective and enthusiasm that are already inspiring our Division of Cognitive and Behavioral Neurology to move in new directions. I am in debt to each of you for helping to keep our research on track while I was pulled away by this manuscript. Also, thank you to Jennifer Woehr, Psy.D., and Ahron Friedberg, M.D., for their invaluable assistance in working through many of my thoughts related to the overall concept of the manuscript. Indeed, the foundation of this manuscript was based on a paper I presented years ago at the Annual American Psychoanalytic Association's Winter Conference at Ari's encouragement.

Thank you to my academic mentors Marcel Kinsbourne, M.D., McWelling Todman, Ph.D., Arien Mack, Ph.D., William Hirst, Ph.D., Arther Dell Orto, Ph.D., and David Silbersweig, M.D. A special thank you to my mentor Dan Simons, Ph.D., who since my time at Harvard University has not only taught me the worth of an academic career but also the true value of being a mentor to others.

Thank you to my parents; my sister, Susan; and her husband, Howard. Thank you to Donna and Allan Essenfeld. Special thanks to my wife, Jenifer, and our children, Sydney and Mathieu. I've heard we are toughest on those we care about the most, and they have all certainly had to make their share of sacrifices throughout this process.

Finally, thank you to my patients, many of whom have worked very hard to become the people they are today. Any inspiration to be found in this book's stories ultimately belongs to them.

Unleash Your Dreams

The Gorilla in the Room

There is none so blind as they that won't see.

—Jonathan Swift

If I hadn't seen it myself, I would never have believed it.

Almost two hundred Harvard students were shown a Quicktime movie in which two sets of players pass basketballs back and forth. Half the players wear white T-shirts; the other half wear black. Students were told to count the number of times the white team passes the ball.

The movie began. The students squinted at the screen, counting silently. Thirty seconds later, the movie stopped. I asked how many passes were counted and duly noted the answer. Then I asked the question that was the real focus of the study: "Did you notice anything unusual?"

Almost 90 percent of the students were surprised by the question. "What do you mean, did I notice anything unusual?" one asked. Their focus was on counting the number of passes, which they did. What else was there to notice?

I played the movie again. "Just watch," I said. "See what you notice when you're not trying to complete a task."

And then it happens. About ten seconds after the tape begins, someone wearing a huge black gorilla costume enters the scene. The "gorilla" walks right into the center of the basketball teams, stops, looks into the camera, thumps its chest, and walks out of the frame. For nine seconds, there was a gorilla in the room—and the vast majority of those who watched the movie didn't have the slightest idea. Only when they watched the movie a second time, with no particular agenda, did they see the gorilla—and burst into laughter.

This phenomenon is known as *inattentional blindness*: the inability to see what we're not attending to. The gorilla wasn't hard to see—quite the contrary—unless you were directing your attention to another task. Then you might miss even something as distinctive as a gorilla in the room.

I wasn't present at the original running of this groundbreaking experiment by my mentor and teacher Daniel J. Simons and his colleague Christopher F. Chabris. But my own work in perception was part of the research that Dan and Chris relied on. And I've shown the images to a number of students, friends, and colleagues (available at http://viscog.beckman.uiuc.edu/media/silverman .html). Every time the result is the same. People don't see what's right in front of them—even something as obvious as a gorilla in the room—because their attention is all bound up in what they're supposed to be looking at.

As a neuroscientist, I've conducted my own research into inattentional blindness, and I've studied a number of other ways that our emotional life affects the workings of our brain. This knowledge has served me well in my work as a psychotherapist, where virtually every day I hear about the ways in which people don't see what's right in front of them.

Take my patient Miriam, a lovely, self-confident woman whom I had seen turn heads just by walking into my waiting room. She had come to me because of her frustrations with romance. "Sure, I can always get a date," she'd told me. "And if I want sex, well, not to brag, but I kind of have my choice of guys. But only guys I don't really like." If a man was "unavailable," a Don Juan, or congenitally unable to commit, Miriam could get him into bed. If he seemed like marriage material, the relationship had a mysterious way of not working out.

Although Miriam didn't know what the solution was, she thought the problem was simple: what could she do to get herself into a good relationship? From my point of view, the problem was more complex. Although Miriam said she wanted a good relationship, I wasn't so sure. I thought perhaps that part of her was deliberately—though unknowingly—trying to sabotage any relationship that might actually make her happy. Miriam wasn't trying to find a good relationship and failing. She was trying to avoid a good relationship—and succeeding.

Certainly, part of Miriam did want a good relationship. But another part seemed determined to avoid even the possibility of a happy, stable marriage. In my view, Miriam's hidden fears had led her to sabotage her progress toward the life she really wanted. It was as though she had gotten into a car, started the engine—and put the emergency brake on. No matter how hard she pressed on the accelerator, that brake was there, holding her back.

When I gently raised this possibility with Miriam, she looked stricken. "But why would I do something like that to myself?" she asked me. "Why would I keep myself from getting what I really want?"

As we worked together, Miriam came to see that her mother, divorced when she was only five, had silently but effectively communicated a powerful sense of envy to her daughter. Unable to stay married to her own husband, Miriam's mother had conveyed the message that Miriam was doomed to the same fate. Miriam felt her mother would be hurt—devastated, in fact—if Miriam were to marry a man she really liked, someone who was ready to commit to her for the long haul.

Indeed, when I asked Miriam about how her romantic success might affect her mother, Miriam's face filled with distress. "It would be like telling Mom what a failure she was—like rubbing her nose in it," Miriam said. "How could I do that to her?"

As we talked further, Miriam came to see that guilt was only part of the story. When Miriam's mother felt envious, she'd found ways of striking out at her daughter. These little blows were often subtle, and probably neither woman realized consciously what was really happening, but on an unconscious level, the message got through loud and clear. For example, Miriam recalled that when she'd started dating her first boyfriend in middle school, she and her mother had begun fighting more. It was always about little things—Miriam's allowance, or her chores, or her schoolwork—but Miriam felt that suddenly her mother just didn't like her as much.

Miriam and her mother had always been close, and Miriam felt her mother's rejection keenly. When Miriam and her boyfriend broke up, her mother really came through for her, comforting her and promising that she'd soon find someone just as good. But when this same pattern was repeated throughout her high school and college years, some part of Miriam understood: to be happy with a guy was to hurt her mother and to risk forfeiting her mother's love. So even though Miriam wanted a good relationship, she was held back by her hidden fears: of guilt, her mother's envy, and the isolation she expected would result from her mother's rejection.

Miriam genuinely wanted a loving, stable relationship. But she also feared it. True, Miriam had kept her fears well hidden, especially from herself. When I raised the possibility that she was deliberately, though unconsciously, avoiding a good relationship, Miriam didn't even understand what I was talking about—at least not on a conscious level. But I could see that on some other level, Miriam sought to reconcile desire and fear by driving with the emergency brake on—pursuing a relationship in a way that was guaranteed to fail.

How could Miriam remain unaware of her self-sabotaging behavior? That's where inattentional blindness comes in. Like the students in Dan's experiment, Miriam kept herself so busy with her appointed task—trying to wrest a commitment from a string of unavailable men—that she couldn't see what was right in front of her. Preoccupied with one relationship drama after another, Miriam never noticed the gorilla in the room.

Paul was also failing to attend to crucial aspects of his life: a hidden fear of disappointing his family and a buried dream of the life he really wanted. A highly effective trial lawyer, Paul had never quite managed to make partner at his prestigious firm. He'd come to me because he knew I worked with athletes, and he thought I could help him to get his game on. "At key moments, I just lose focus," he told me. "I know I'm a good lawyer—certainly I'm as good as any of the guys who made partner this year. But somehow they've made it and I haven't."

Like Miriam, Paul was bewildered by his failure in an arena where he ought to have been successful. Like Miriam, he believed he'd been working wholeheartedly toward his goal. But, like Miriam, I thought he might be ignoring the gorilla in the room.

"What do you think your life as partner would be like?" I asked one day.

Paul frowned. "Well, I'd make a lot more money—which I could certainly use," he said. "People would look up to me. I'd get the really big cases—the ones everyone wants. And I'd feel secure, you know. Like I'd finally made something of myself."

I couldn't help noticing that the longer Paul spoke, the more unhappy and frustrated he seemed to be. "Anything else?" I prompted.

"Of course, I'd have to take this job more seriously than I have been," he said slowly. "I mean, partner—that's a real commitment. I wouldn't just be working for myself. I'd have a real stake in how the firm did. If we had a bad year or two, it wouldn't just be somebody else's problem. It also would be my problem—my responsibility. If we had to lay people off, fire people—at least some of that would be on me."

Paul's frown deepened. "I'd have to make sure to bring in the big-money clients—the ones who could really keep us going," he said. "I'm a good lawyer but I'm not such a good rainmaker. I'd have to put a lot more effort into getting us that business—mental effort, emotional effort, time. I wouldn't feel as though I was ever off duty."

The more we talked, the clearer it became to both of us: Paul didn't really want to do the kind of work or take the financial responsibility that being partner would entail. With great effort, he might be capable of doing that kind of work, but it wasn't where his heart lay. Although he liked law, what Paul really loved was music, and as we worked together, he began to realize that his dream life would be to put in a forty-hour week at a secure job that he enjoyed—but also to become a serious amateur musician who played chamber music each week and occasionally performed.

Why hadn't Paul pursued such a life right out of college? Paul explained that his family had scrimped and saved to send him to the best schools, and that he was the first person in his family to even attend college. He felt he owed it to his family to make good in the clearest, most obvious way, by rising to the very top of his profession. He didn't think they'd understand his decision to pursue a hobby in music, let alone respect it.

As I saw it, Paul was wrestling with a number of issues: a buried dream about the kind of life he wanted along with hidden fears of guilt, isolation, and being trapped in a false dream. He also feared not being a real man, in either his own or his family's eyes: what kind of man turns down top dollar in a prestigious job to play the violin? Desiring a calmer, more artistic life but fearing to claim it, Paul ignored his hidden dream to focus on his appointed task: lobbying to make partner. Yet because his heart wasn't in it—

because he really dreaded the goal he said he wanted—he had to find some way to trip himself up. It was as though he diligently arranged his books and papers on the table—but as soon as he sat down to work, the gorilla starting flinging them around the room. Of course he couldn't keep his focus!

Paul had tried to solve his problem by working harder, but that only made things worse: the harder he worked, the more agitated his gorilla became. Not being able to concentrate raised Paul's anxiety levels, which provoked him to work harder still.

Paul's situation had all the makings of a vicious circle. Until he attended to his hidden fears and buried dreams, he'd never understand why his career kept stalling out.

Paul is still working out the financial and logistical details of how to achieve his dream. But in coming to terms with his true feelings and his true vision, he was able to stop his futile efforts to create a life he didn't really want. Paul still isn't sure how he's going to make his dream come true. But now that he's working wholeheartedly to get the life he really wants, the gorilla in the room has stopped making mischief.

Hidden Fears and Buried Dreams

I work with many different types of patients, from world-famous athletes and performers to men and women who are simply pursuing their quest for meaningful work and satisfying love. At all levels of achievement, I've noticed many people struggling with the same hidden fears and buried dreams that plagued Paul and Miriam. Their desires seem to point one way, but their actions lead another. They tell you what they want, but they don't seem genuinely committed to getting it. They focus on the day-to-day actions they think will bring them happiness—the perpetual tug-of-war with a lover who won't commit, the demanding workload involved in becoming partner—but they never quite achieve what they set out to do. And they are unaware of their own unconscious efforts to sabotage their progress.

In some cases, my patients really do want what they say they want. Miriam, for example, genuinely wanted a good relationship. As she came to realize how her fears were holding her back, she was able to work on resolving those fears and laying them to rest. She could go on to pursue the stable, committed relationship that really was going to make her happy.

Sometimes a person's dream is genuinely difficult to fulfill. Jenna, for example, had come to me out of frustration over the constant setbacks in her advertising career. Despite her widely acknowledged brilliance and her many awards, Jenna had never gotten the promotions she knew she deserved. A smart, competent woman whom everybody liked, Jenna was ignoring what should have been obvious—her tendencies to unerringly choose the wrong side in office politics and to become enmeshed in petty feuds and power struggles. Although Jenna realized that her relationships with her coworkers were often in turmoil, she thought it was just something that happened, not a dynamic for which she had any responsibility.

Not until she started working with me did Jenna realize that she'd never really liked advertising, despite her obvious talent for it—and that her dislike for her profession was probably related to her constant involvement in office feuds and battles. "If I had my life to do over again," she told me one day, "I'd be a doctor." Fear—of her father's envy, her brother's resentment, being seen as unfeminine and too ambitious—had held her back. Never facing her fears, Jenna had been controlled by them, without the chance to examine how rational they were or how much they mattered to her.

But by the time Jenna saw things clearly, she was in her early forties. Now she faces a difficult choice: enter a lengthy training period that she won't complete until she's past fifty, come to terms with her current profession, or find some other work that might satisfy her interest in health and healing. She still hasn't decided how best to reshape her life, but at least she's no longer setting herself up for failure.

My Encounter with the Gorilla

I haven't only watched my patients struggle with the gorilla; I've also had to contend with some hidden fears and buried dreams of my own. After completing a master's degree, I landed a good job in a growing health-care organization where, after only two years, I was offered a significant promotion. Not only would my new position give me more income and greater responsibility, it also would put me in line for a much larger role in shaping the growth of a successful company that was soon to go public. It seemed like an incredible opportunity, but I wasn't sure I wanted a lifetime career in administration. What was I going to do?

When I finally turned the promotion down, I seized upon the only possibility I saw as equivalent: medical school. After all, I was interested in anatomy and biochemistry, I was smart and competent, and I'd always been a good student. The prospect of medical school seemed certain to reassure my family, who were understandably concerned about my having turned down such a good job. And who's more prestigious, legitimate, and successful than a doctor?

Relieved at having settled my future so effectively, I won entry into a transitional program at Tufts University. As soon as I successfully completed the preliminary coursework, I'd go on to study at one of the most prestigious med schools in the country.

Then I hit a wall. All through college, I'd been dedicated, determined, well prepared. I'd never turned in a paper even one day late, never had serious trouble studying for a test. Now my concentration seemed to have evaporated. I just couldn't master the course material, and I couldn't understand why.

Someone suggested that I go to Powell Associates, a professional testing group in nearby Cambridge, Massachusetts. (They were the company that helped NASA select the astronauts who were slated to go to the moon.) So I made an appointment and took all the tests they gave me—IQ, aptitude, every sort of assessment that this cutting-edge company had devised. I fully expected to discover that I didn't have the right kind of mind to become a doctor, but instead I found out just the opposite. Not only did I possess the necessary intelligence to enter this challenging career, I'd also scored above the general norm of intelligence for people who already were physicians. There was no learning disability to explain my mysterious failure, no objective reason why I shouldn't have been able to get the work done. I just couldn't do it.

Someone at Powell thought therapy might be helpful, and so, obediently, I started going to weekly sessions. One day, my therapist looked me in the eye. "Did you ever think you may not really want to go to medical school?" he asked me. "That maybe you're sabotaging yourself because you don't really want to do this?"

No, I realized. I didn't want to do this. I'd turned to medical school in desperation, just to have something prestigious and successful to work for. But I didn't really want to be a doctor. I didn't know what I wanted to be.

Then I did something that might seem absurd—and yet for me it made tremendous sense: I joined the Israeli Army. I knew I wasn't going to settle in Israel or make a permanent career in the military. I just needed something meaningful to do while I figured out the rest of my life.

It turned out to be the best choice I could have made. I ended up living in an apartment in Tel Aviv, spending hours, days, whole weeks by myself, free of any outside pressures from teachers, friends, or family. Without anyone to make suggestions or offer advice, I started thinking for myself about what my skills were, what I was really good at—what I truly loved.

Slowly, very slowly, I began to see a pattern. When I'd been an undergraduate, I'd had a minor in research. I'd also been a teaching assistant for a research course. For a while, I'd worked at a radio station—where I'd been the research director charged with discovering what kinds of programming the listeners preferred. Clearly, I loved research. And the human brain had always fascinated me.

Finally, everything clicked: I would go on to graduate school in neuroscience and cognitive psychology, studying the mysteries of the human brain. And because I liked helping people, I'd also learn about the various types of psychotherapy. My graduate degree would enable me to become a scientist, a researcher, and a therapist. I returned to the United States, empowered to pursue this newer, truer dream.

When I finally did become a psychotherapist, I assumed my job was to help people find the happiness they sought—in love, in work, in their personal lives. I soon realized, however, that people frequently encounter deep conflicts over happiness itself. Just when they seem on the verge of getting what they've always wanted, the self-sabotage begins: mysterious patterns of illness, injury, lateness; sudden quarrels at work or at home; obstacles and setbacks that seem accidental but that somehow prevent people from achieving—or at least from enjoying—their fulfillment in work, love, or personal life.

I remember the first time I really noticed this pattern. I was doing postgraduate work at Cornell University Medical College while treating a professional athlete, a man literally at the top of his game. Yet he'd come to me because he'd been in a slump for several weeks, an inexplicable falling off of his previously superb performance.

I could think of only one way to explain this mysterious slump. This man had to be sabotaging himself, setting himself up for failure because of his own hidden fears about success. Yet I couldn't quite believe my own analysis. Surely someone who had worked so hard for his success would not have so much trouble enjoying it when it came?

So I turned to a senior colleague for help. "Oh, sure," my colleague said immediately. "Lots of people struggle with that." He hunted briefly for something on his desk and then handed me a copy of Sigmund Freud's 1916 paper "Those Wrecked by Success."

Since Freud was the founder of psychoanalysis, I was naturally eager to read what he'd written. In this groundbreaking paper, the pioneering analyst explored the difficulty some people have in enjoying the happiness they've worked so hard for. People even became ill, he wrote, "precisely when a deeply rooted and long-cherished wish has come to fulfillment. It seems then as though they were not able to tolerate their happiness."

Not able to tolerate their happiness. That seemed a perfect description of the athlete I was treating. He had worked all his life to become a star player, and now that he was one, he couldn't seem to tolerate it. But why? Why couldn't he enjoy his success?

Freud himself had to struggle to understand it. He was so perplexed that he looked not to science but to literature, citing plays of Shakespeare and Ibsen. Relying on those playwrights' insights into human behavior, Freud came to a fascinating conclusion: resistance to happiness is caused by the guilty pangs of conscience. The characters he studied had all wished for something they believed was wrong—an affair with a married man or the murder of an elderly king. They were comfortable wishing for this illicit pleasure; maybe they could even bring themselves to work for it. But once they were actively engaged in the affair or sitting on the throne, they felt guilty about what they'd done to get there.

I was intrigued by this analysis, and it seemed to apply to many people I knew, including my patient: he felt guilty about outdoing the team captain, who happened to be having a bad year. In my view, my patient hadn't done anything wrong, but he felt guilty all the same. Likewise, Miriam guiltily believed that achieving her own happy marriage would make her mother feel worse about her divorce, just as Paul felt guilty about not fulfilling his family's dreams.

But fear of guilt wasn't the only issue driving my patients. Some of them feared envy, much as Miriam did, along with the isolation that might result from being rejected by an envious person. Some patients feared their own anger at the parents who had pushed them too hard or had made their love conditional on achievement. Instead of facing these painful feelings, a patient might become mysteriously unable to succeed, an unconscious expression of hidden rage at the parents who seemed to overvalue their success.

Some patients, like Paul, feared choosing options that seemed to make them less of a man or less of a woman. And, like Paul, many feared being trapped in a false dream, sabotaging their progress toward a goal they never really wanted.

Claiming the Life You Really Want

If you're ready to claim the life you really want, I offer you a three-step plan for getting in touch with your desires, facing your hidden fears, and deciding what matters most to you. Following this plan may not always be easy. But the plan itself is simple. You just need to pay attention to the gorilla in the room, and understand what you really want and what you're really doing.

Step 1: Uncover Your Dreams

So often, we don't know what we really want. We're just going along on automatic pilot, following the path that everyone else thinks will make us happy. Maybe we're following our family's advice. Perhaps we're caught up in the fantasies and values of our culture—the picture-book marriage, the successful career. We might even be pursuing a childhood dream without realizing how far we've outgrown it.

Your first step in claiming the life you want is to get in touch with your own desires, defining your dreams, goals, and wishes in your own terms. There's a tremendous power in accessing your true intentions, and in part one of this book, I'll help you do just that.

Step 2: Identify Your Hidden Fears

A few students in the Harvard study might have been embarrassed by missing the gorilla, but no one really suffered by not being aware of its presence. Alas, that's not true of your gorilla in the room—the self-sabotaging behavior that is keeping you from what you really want. This kind of behavior is usually driven by fear, so in step 2 you'll have a chance to look at the role fear plays in your life, and you'll find out the fears that are affecting you the most.

Step 3: Decide What Matters Most

Having identified your fears, you need to determine just how realistic they are. Will making a good living really turn you into the heartless rich person your family has always despised? Will marriage really entrap you in a life you don't want? Will success—in work, love, or your personal life—really provoke the envy of your loved ones?

You also need to look clearly at your buried dreams. What would it take to fulfill them now? How much effort and sacrifice would really be required—more than you've feared? Less than you've feared? Maybe you have some options now that you didn't have when you first buried those dreams. Perhaps some compromises or new possibilities will become evident, paths you couldn't see when you were busy telling yourself "I can't have that—it's not for me."

Once you've taken a clear, realistic look at your situation, you have the opportunity to choose the goals you wholeheartedly want to pursue. Having analyzed whether your fears have a realistic basis, you can then decide whether they matter more than the desires you've finally connected with. Perhaps making a lot of money will separate you from your family; would you still rather have the money? Perhaps some friends will envy your newfound success at work; does their envy mean more to you than your own dreams?

You, too, can get in touch with your buried dreams while identifying, analyzing, and overcoming your fears. Welcome to a whole new world—one where you pay attention to what really matters.

PART ONE

Uncover Your Dreams

CHAPTER 1

Know Your Own Mind—
Even if It Scares You

Have you ever tried and tried and tried to fall asleep . . . and the harder you try, the more awake you feel?

Or perhaps you've had the experience of telling yourself not to bring up a difficult topic—your best friend's bad haircut or your boss's recent divorce—and then hearing yourself blurt out the very comment you're desperate to avoid?

How about that disturbing encounter—tomorrow's job interview or last night's disastrous date—that you're determined not to think about? Does every effort to divert your thoughts simply increase your obsession?

If any of these examples rings a bell with you, then you've experienced one of the most interesting—and frustrating—aspects of the human mind, what fellow neuroscientist Daniel W. Wegner calls the "ironic processes of mental control." Dan described these processes in a groundbreaking article in *Psychological Review* that helped to inspire my own work in this fascinating field.

Although ironic processes don't tell the whole story of buried dreams and hidden fears, they're an extremely important part of knowing our own mind. Whether we're talking about falling asleep, sticking to a diet, getting over a fight, or following a dream, we need to understand how ironic processes work, because they're one of the most common methods our mind uses to keep us from getting what we really want.

How Your Mind Secretly Undermines You

Let's suppose you're concentrating on accomplishing a specific goal. You may be trying to perform a physical action: *Don't hit the golf ball into the sand trap*; or *Don't run over that broken bottle in the middle of the road*. You may want to exert some control over your body itself: *Fall asleep*; or *Stop feeling nauseated!* You might be trying to influence your actions in a social situation: *Don't mention colleges—George's son just got rejected by his top three choices*; or *Don't tell Sue that secret!* You may even be trying to direct your mind's own thoughts and feelings: *Stop waiting for that new guy to call*; or *Don't think any more about that awful fight with Mom*.

Although these are all actions that we are presumably capable of completing successfully, we tend to fail at many of them—often. Indeed, sometimes it seems that the more we don't want to do something—stay awake, blurt out a secret, obsess about romance—the more we feel compelled to do it.

I work with a number of professional athletes, and they are especially aware of this frustrating lack of control. If a baseball player is in a slump, for example, he is likely to obsess about his inability to hit the ball. Every time he comes up to bat, he worries about whether he'll get a hit—and the more he worries, the less

likely he is to get one. Or a pro golfer who's had bad luck on a particular hole during a tournament often gets spooked when she has
to play that hole again. She remembers all the mistakes she made
the last time—and then labors under what feels like an irresistible compulsion to repeat them. Athletes from all different types of
sports describe the same phenomenon: "The harder I try to avoid
a mistake, the more inevitable that mistake starts to feel."

Sports psychologists and coaches often try to help by telling
players to relax when they tee up or come to bat. But for many
athletes, these new instructions only seem to make the problem
worse. "Relax, relax, relax," they repeat to themselves, becoming
tenser and less confident with every word.

Dan's article brilliantly illuminates the problem: our mental
control is by nature divided. One aspect of our mind, the Operator, tries to do what we want. Another aspect, the Monitor, tries to
find out whether we've done it.

On the surface, this would seem like a logical arrangement.
After all, you don't need to keep trying to fall asleep once you've
already fallen asleep. You don't need to keep diverting your
thoughts away from an unpleasant topic after they've already
been diverted. And you don't need to keep avoiding a mistake
after you've successfully avoided it. In fact, it's crucial for every
function to have not just an on switch ("Do this") but also an off
switch ("Okay, you've succeeded; you can stop now"). Otherwise
we'd be like the broom in "The Sorcerer's Apprentice," bringing
bucket after bucket of water when the tub was already full. So our
Monitor's job is to notify us when our task has been completed,
freeing us to turn off the switch and proceed to the next task.

But how does the Monitor know whether our task has been
completed? Alas, that's where so many of us undermine ourselves.
By nature, the Monitor isn't set up to seek evidence that we have
done something. Instead, it looks for evidence that we haven't.
If it finds no evidence to the contrary, we've succeeded, and we
can move on to new activities. But if our Monitor finds any evidence

of any remaining problem, we'll stay stuck in our same old task.

Here's a somewhat simplified version of how our Operator and our Monitor interact so that ironically we end up doing exactly the opposite of what we intended:

Operator: "I'd like to go to sleep now. So I'm going to try to go to sleep. Okay, can I stop trying? Am I asleep yet?"

Monitor: "Wait, let me check. Nope, still awake . . . still awake . . . still awake."

Operator: "Last time I did this task, I made a mistake, and I really don't want to make it again. Am I successfully avoiding my past mistake?"

Monitor: "To answer that question, I'm going to seek out all available evidence that you are *not* avoiding your past mistake. Wow, look at all this evidence I've found! And guess what? The more evidence I look for, the more I find!" (Oops. Now all you can think about is that mistake and all the possible ways you might repeat it. From being a tiny, nagging fear, your concern with that mistake has blossomed into a full-blown obsession.)

Operator: "That fight I had with Mom last week is still bothering me—I really want to stop thinking about it. Have I succeeded yet? Can I stop trying to stop?"

Monitor: "To answer that question, I have to look for every shred of evidence that you are still thinking about that fight. If I don't find any, then you've been successful. But if I find even the tiniest sign that you're still thinking about Mom, you'll have to keep trying to stop—while I keep seeking evidence." (You guessed it. As your Monitor continues its ironic process, that fight with Mom begins to completely dominate your thoughts. "Am I still thinking about it now? Now? Now?" "Yes, yes, yes—more than ever!")

You see the problem. Some instructions—*relax, avoid, don't make a mistake*—are virtually impossible to complete because of that inevitable monitoring process. Thinking about the problem reactivates the problem, a seemingly endless feedback loop that locks us into a permanent cycle of repeating our mistakes and obsessing about our failures.

But here's the good news. This version of getting in our own way is not necessarily due to buried dreams or hidden fears. We're not deliberately sabotaging our own progress, we're just not doing a very good job of pursuing our goals. So if your only problem is those pesky ironic processes, consider yourself lucky: I'm about to share an easy way to free yourself from this mental trap.

Think Positive

Athletes and their coaches were among the first to discover the secret I'm about to share, one that sports psychologists and other cognitive scientists have also helped promote: give your mind only positive instruction . . . and then imagine that your success has already happened.

In other words, don't tell yourself not to miss the ball. Don't even tell yourself to hit the ball. Instead, imagine that you have already hit the ball—and then put yourself into the mental state you'd be in if you actually had hit it. In effect, you'll have fooled your Monitor, which won't be able to find any negative evidence that you're about to repeat your same old failure. By convincing yourself that you already are successful, you will succeed.

Likewise, don't tell yourself to fall asleep. I know that sounds like a positive instruction, but it still prompts your Monitor to look for evidence of wakefulness. Instead, visualize yourself already asleep, or simply imagine yourself relaxed, happy, and at peace. Don't focus on trying to sleep—instead, try to remember in luxurious, minute detail exactly what it feels like to be sleepy. If you can, enjoy the process.

Another approach to a demanding task is not to think about the task at all. If, for example, you want to sleep, ask your mind to daydream about a task that you find pleasant and soothing—your own personal equivalent of counting sheep—with no goal, no expectations, just a pleasant state of interest. Replay the plot of a movie you loved. Daydream about your next vacation. Relive one of your favorite romantic moments. Without any goal at which you can succeed or fail, you'll fool your Monitor into thinking it has nothing to do, and your own natural tiredness will take over. (By the way, don't try counting sheep—that actually gives you an impossible-to-achieve goal that tends to keep you up and make you tense!)

My patient Barb, a marketing executive, found positive thinking extremely helpful in improving her performance at work. Barb had always had trouble speaking in public, and she was especially

---

SCIENCE MATTERS

Sleep without Sheep

There actually is a study showing that counting sheep is less effective in combating insomnia than is visualizing a pleasant or soothing scene, such as a holiday, a sunny afternoon, a family Christmas, a walk in a meadow, or a country scene with a waterfall. In 2002, Oxford University researchers Allison G. Harvey and Suzanna Payne decided to test how Dan Wegner's "ironic processes" theory might play out for insomniacs, so they divided forty-one self-identified insomniacs into three groups: one was given no instructions; the second was simply told to distract themselves by, for example, counting sheep; and the third was told to visualize a pleasant or soothing scene such as a waterfall. Although people in the "general distraction" group found that counting sheep was better than doing nothing at all, the "imagery distraction" group were the clear winners, falling asleep significantly sooner than the other two groups.

concerned about her difficulty now that her job required her to make weekly presentations to her boss and his colleagues. She felt the first few presentations hadn't gone well, and since she genuinely wanted to succeed at her job, she came to me for help.

With my coaching, Barb began to visualize her success. She imagined herself speaking fluently, clearly, effectively. She pictured how good it would feel to present a speech with authority, to answer questions without hesitation, to remain in command of the room. Barb found these fantasies thrilling, and they did indeed improve her presentations. Because Barb had no conflicts about doing well at work—because she genuinely wanted to make good speeches—this technique worked for her.

Many of us believe that the way to improve our performance is to monitor it consciously. When we do well, we say to ourselves, "Good for me!" When we do badly, we tell ourselves, "That was a mistake; I should have done such-and-such instead." We believe that through this process of continual evaluation, we'll improve our game, our speaking ability, or any other activity that matters to us.

In fact, that kind of evaluation has its place, but only after the fact. While you are playing, speaking, writing, or otherwise engaged in a demanding activity, it's far more helpful to give yourself constant praise, even when you do something wrong. "Good for me! Look how hard I'm trying! Look how much I'm learning! I have so much to be proud of!" Afterward you can say, "Wow, I'll never use that joke again," or "I wonder whether it would have been more effective to feint right instead of to charge left." But making any kind of judgment during play only activates your Monitor, who then begins searching for every shred of evidence that you're doing everything wrong.

If you'd like to experience the power of positive thinking, try the following exercise. I've presented it with a work example, but it works just as well with regard to love (such as visualizing a successful date or sexual encounter) and personal life (for example, visualizing a graceful, dignified, and assertive response to family

SCIENCE MATTERS

Rewiring Your Brain

Throughout this book, I'll be helping you use visualization and guided imagery as a transformational tool. That's because visualizing an action can affect your brain in virtually the same way as physically performing it, creating new synapses and pathways. According to Harvard neuroscientist Steve Kosslyn, visualizing yourself performing a skill actually helps you improve that skill: "For example, if you were learning a new dance, visualizing the steps would lead you to be a better dancer—provided that imagined practice is intermixed with actual practice."

Dr. Kosslyn's conclusion is partly based on research by Gayle Deutsch and her colleagues, who found that when experimental subjects were asked to visualize an action—rotating an imaginary object—they activated the same parts of the brain that are used to physically perform the same action (specifically the parietal and frontal lobes of the right hemisphere). Dr. Kosslyn's colleague neuroscientist Marc Jeannerod, took this idea one step farther: he says that imagining an action creates memories that are similar or perhaps even identical to memories of actually performing the action, and these memories can be used to help you perform the action the next time, just as if you'd actually been practicing it physically. Once you actually do perform it physically, real-life memories supersede the ones created by the visualization. But until then, visualizing your ideal performance of an activity—succeeding at whatever you've chosen to imagine—really does count as practice in doing something well.

In other words, visualization isn't just mind over matter. It's actually mind creating matter as your images literally alter your brain.

members). I've suggested one approach to visualization, but feel free to experiment with your own variations and approaches. Just make sure your focus is on visualizing a success as if it has already happened. Don't give yourself any opportunity to monitor or evaluate your performance. That ironic Monitor will trip you up every time!

EXERCISE
Visualize Success

1. *Relax.* This exercise works best if you're in a calm, relaxed frame of mind, so take a few moments to breathe deeply and allow your mind to clear. Take ten slow, deep breaths, breathing in on a count of 8 and out on a count of 8. (If you find it difficult to breathe so slowly, begin with a count of 2, then 4, then 6, then 8—then try ten deep breaths on a count of 8.) Focusing entirely on counting your breaths will help relax your body and clear your mind, putting you into a receptive state for the rest of the exercise.

2. *Visualize yourself proceeding through the activity of your choice.* If, like Barb, you want to improve your public speaking, begin visualizing the activity from the very beginning. See yourself entering the room where the talk will be given. Imagine yourself speaking. Hear how clear your words are, how forceful. Notice the facial expressions on your audience. Bring your visualization into sharp focus by paying attention to specific sensory details. Ask yourself what you see, hear, taste, smell, and feel. Experience the bright yellow of the wall, the sounds of the traffic coming through the open window, the scent of the coffee, the feel of the pencil between your fingers, and the sensation of your wool blazer against your skin. If you don't know the sensory details of the actual place you'll be giving the speech, make them up.

Sensory experience—even imaginary experience—will make your visualization feel more real to you, and that sense of reality will support your sense of confidence and well-being.

3. *See your activity ending.* Give your visualization a more "finished" sense by proceeding on, through the end of your activity. See yourself finishing your speech, picking up your notes, putting them into your briefcase. Notice the response of your audience. Again, make it as specific as possible—see as many individual faces as you can bring into your mental vision, noticing their expressions, hearing any words that might be spoken. Find a satisfying way to bring your visualized experience to a close. Take a few moments to savor your success.

4. *Remain in your relaxed state for another few minutes.* Finish with another ten slow, deep breaths, inhaling on a count of 8 and exhaling on a count of 8. Try to focus entirely on your breathing. This "mind-clearing" time will also help you retain the emotional aura of your visualization and will ensure that you don't erase its good effects by jumping right back into an anxious, busy state.

5. *Jot down a few notes to yourself.* Many people find it helpful to take a few more minutes to describe their experience in writing or to note the main points they wish to take away from their visualization. Writing down your feelings, thoughts, and conclusions can be a terrific way to give form to your experience, which in turn will help you remember it longer.

The Limits of Positive Thinking

I'm all for positive thinking, but it does have its limits. If, like many of my patients, you are driven by hidden fears and buried dreams, positive thinking probably won't work. That's because, no matter what you think you're doing, you're ignoring the real intentions that are driving your actions. Divided against yourself, you're not entirely sure you want to achieve your chosen result, so you have no genuine commitment to positive thinking. In fact, I would go so far as to say that if positive thinking fails you, that's a pretty good indication that there's some hidden fear or buried dream that you have consciously or unconsciously decided to ignore.

For example, suppose, like my patient Teresa, you are having trouble with your career. Teresa was no stranger to positive thinking. A brilliant tennis player, she had recently turned pro after a dazzling amateur career. She'd picked up her first tennis racket at age three and now, nearly twenty years later, she was approaching the pinnacle of her success. Visualization and positive thinking had helped to put her there.

Recently, she had been plagued by a series of small injuries—a pulled ligament, a bruised shoulder, once even a severe sprain that kept her out of a match she'd spent months training for. Injuries are common among athletes, and at first Teresa had written off the incidents as a run of bad luck. But when they caused her to miss her third match in a row, her trainer suggested that she talk to me.

"What do you think the problem is?" I asked Teresa when we first met.

She shook her head, barely able to hold back the tears. "I'm used to working hard for what I want—and I'm used to winning. But this is something I'm doing to myself. I know I'm the one holding myself back. But I can't figure out why."

Clearly, Teresa was willing to work hard for what she wanted. No one becomes a topflight tennis pro without unremitting work and passionate ambition. Teresa had been blessed with talent, drive, and a positive attitude, and she was finally on the verge of achieving her lifelong dream. Her goal was practically within her grasp, so why balk now?

Gradually we discovered that Teresa had always longed for

a close group of friends. She'd come from a cold, withholding family who had pushed her to achieve her athletic goals without giving her much emotional support. Her dedication to tennis had isolated her from other girls her age and hadn't left her much time for a social life with boys, either. The first time she ever felt like she belonged was on the circuit, hanging out with the other tennis players who shared her dedication and love of the game.

But Teresa's friends were also her rivals. If she truly became the number-one champion, she couldn't expect to stay close to numbers two, three, and four. For Teresa, becoming a success meant losing the only friends she'd ever had.

Although most women don't become star athletes, I've met many who shared Teresa's fears of isolation. "Once I'm successful, everyone will hate me," another patient once told me, a high-powered advertising executive who had suddenly found herself feeling unmotivated and listless. "My husband is already angry that I'm spending so much time at work, and my sister is always making these little digs about my fancy career. My best friend quit her job two years ago to stay home with her kids—we're still close but I'm always worried that she'll look down on me for being a bad mother, or worse, that she'll feel threatened by my choice. I've worked all my life to get to this level—but what's the point if I have no one to share it with?"

Like that patient and many others, Teresa was holding herself back because of her hidden fears. Part of her wanted to become a champion. But part of her feared losing her circle of friends—a conflict too deep for mere positive thinking to resolve. Teresa's fear of isolation was the part of her experience she just couldn't bear to attend to.

Is There Something Your're Ignoring?

If positive thinking has worked for you, congratulations! But if you want to take a deeper look, let's get started. In this section you'll have the chance to find out whether hidden fears and buried dreams are interfering with your progress—whether you, too, are ignoring a hidden pattern of self-sabotage.

Let me be very clear: I am not saying that fear itself is the problem. Fear can often be a healthy emotion, one that warns us about dangers we need to avoid. And even if you think your fears are giving you faulty information ("Everybody will hate me!" "I'll never find true love!" "My family will abandon me and I'll be all alone forever!"), those fears needn't hold you back. Most people who achieve happy and fulfilling lives will agree that they've often experienced fear, both rational and irrational. The key is learning how to feel your fears and then put them in perspective. Not fear, but hidden fear, is the problem.

Nor am I saying that you must follow every dream. Even the most satisfying life requires some compromise, giving up some dreams to pursue others. Moreover, our dreams change and grow throughout our lives. Changing your mind about what you want and what you're willing to give up is a natural part of growth. Not abandoned dreams but buried dreams are the problem.

That's why getting in touch with hidden fears and buried dreams is key to getting the life you really want. So look at the following checklist and see if any of the items ring any bells. Put a check mark in the box by any item that you think applies to you. Put an X by any item that seems especially true.

CHECKLIST
Am I Holding Myself Back without Realizing It?

☐ I find myself hesitant to share good news with one or more of my loved ones, such as friends, family, romantic partners, or spouse.

☐ My reaction to praise is often to disagree and/or to find some way to compare myself unfavorably to the other person.

- [ ] I frequently feel mystified by why things don't work out for me.

- [ ] I often have difficulty being on time for meetings and/or deadlines. In fact, the more important the meeting or deadline, the harder it is for me to be on time.

- [ ] At work, I often end up on the wrong side of office politics or find myself enmeshed in petty feuds.

- [ ] I've noticed a pattern of things going well—at work, in love, or in my personal life—until out of the blue, something mysteriously disrupts my good time.

- [ ] I've begun to have trouble doing something that formerly came easily to me.

- [ ] I've begun to have trouble getting along with someone I was formerly close to.

- [ ] Whenever I get into a romantic relationship, I notice myself quarreling with my friends or simply liking them less.

- [ ] I often have headaches, stomachaches, backaches, or exhaustion just before or just after a family visit.

- [ ] I start off great at a new job—and then suddenly my rate of progress seems to slow.

- [ ] I have a typical breaking point for relationships, whether after the first date, the first month, or the first two years; I see myself as someone who can't stay in a relationship longer than a certain amount of time.

- [ ] I tend to be interested in romantic partners who are involved with other people.

- [ ] I tend to be interested in romantic partners who are in crisis—unemployed, struggling with an addiction, coping with a family tragedy.

- [ ] I tend to be interested in romantic partners whom I would identify as ambivalent or afraid to commit.

- [ ] My friends have a very different sense of my abilities and/or attractiveness than I do.

- [ ] I frequently engage in activities—personal or professional—while insisting that I am no good at them or will not succeed in my goals.

- [ ] I am critical of most financially successful people, on the grounds that they are either greedy or spiritually limited.

- [ ] I am critical of most married people, on the grounds that they are either shallow or settling.

- [ ] I find myself becoming less interested in friends or romantic partners after they become more happy or successful.

- [ ] I find myself becoming less interested in friends or romantic partners as they become more interested in me.

Now look back over the items you've marked and see if you notice any patterns of self-sabotaging behavior. Pay particular attention to any item that upsets you or makes you anxious. Give even more attention to those you find your mind wandering away from, as when you are bored or distracted. Those feelings are usually good indications that there's something going on that you might want to pay attention to.

Are You Driving with the Emergency Brake On?

Often we claim to be going full speed ahead toward a cherished goal when in fact we're actually driving with the emergency brake on. Despite our lip service to a particular end—marriage, career, family, a happy personal life—we also hold negative opinions that make it difficult to pursue our goals wholeheartedly.

So let's explore your attitudes toward success in work, love, and personal life. Look over the following statements. Check off the ones with which you agree. Put an X beside the ones that seem especially true or powerful.

CHECKLIST
What Do I Think about Success?

☐ People who make lots of money have very little time left in their lives for anything else.

☐ Women who have great careers will face extra challenges finding love.

☐ Women who have great careers will face extra challenges starting a family.

☐ Most people in positions of power are a bit heartless—they have to be, to do those jobs.

☐ It's hard to become successful and remain close to the people who knew you when.

☐ Someone who is happy or content will often be the target of envy.

☐ People for whom things come easily miss out on a very important life lesson.

☐ People who get along with their boss are usually either naive or sucking up.

☐ Becoming successful can really change a person—and rarely for the better.

☐ If I became more successful in work, love, or my personal life, I expect my relationships with my loved ones would change quite a bit.

☐ It's very difficult to become a success without selling out in some way.

☐ A man who is not professionally and financially successful will probably not have a happy emotional or family life either.

☐ If I became more successful at work, I would expect to be less close to my coworkers.

☐ People who are professionally successful find it very difficult to have a happy home life.

☐ People who are successful may be feared, envied, even respected—but they are rarely liked.

☐ Successful or talented people are frequently arrogant.

☐ Being liked is more important than being respected or admired.

☐ When I'm in a good relationship, I tend to lose my edge at work.

☐ Successful or talented people have difficulty relating to "ordinary" people.

☐ A person whose daily life is happy and peaceful is probably shallow or insensitive.

☐ Though most people don't realize it, success is frequently a mixed blessing.

Look back at the items you've checked or starred. Then ask yourself if there is any conflict between the items you've marked and the goals you say you want. Again, conflict isn't the problem; hidden conflict is. For example, most people will agree that it's hard to succeed at work while also raising a family. That's not a hidden conflict, but an open one—even if you don't always know how to resolve it. But if you say you want to earn a lot of money while also believing that rich people are jerks, you may be setting yourself up for failure. Likewise, if you say you want to get married while also believing that most marriages are unhappy, you might be caught in a conflict that is holding you back.

Remember, discovering a conflict doesn't necessarily mean giving up either your beliefs or your goals. Perhaps you'll decide that you will be the exception that proves the rule. Or maybe you can take steps to guard against the outcome you most fear, promising yourself to increase your charitable donations if you become rich or committing to positive efforts to keep your marriage healthy. But you can't take those helpful steps if you're not even aware of the conflicts. As always, awareness is key.

Rediscover Your Buried Dreams

You've had a chance to think about hidden fears. But what about your buried dreams? In this section, I invite you to take a closer look at what you really want, and at what might be holding you back.

As you check out the following questionnaire, remember that there are no right or wrong answers. Your only goal is to become aware of what's going on inside you. I suggest answering each of these questions as quickly as possible, to see what your immediate response is. You may surprise yourself! Then, after you've had a few minutes to sit with the questions, you might return to answer them a second time, more slowly and thoughtfully.

QUESTIONNAIRE
What Do You Want—and What's Holding You Back?

1. When I picture myself in five years, I hope I _____
   _____.

2. The thing I find most frustrating about my life now is _____
   _____.

3. If I could change something about my life now with the wave of a magic wand, it would be _____
   _____.

4. If I could magically change something about my past, it would be _____

_____ .

5. The person who has most helped me get what I want in life is _____ . He/she has helped me by _____

_____ .

6. The person who has made it hardest for me to get what I want in life is _____ . He/she has held me back by _____

_____ .

7. When I picture myself in a great relationship, I imagine _____

_____ .

8. When I picture myself doing great work of some kind, I imagine _____

_____ .

9. When I picture myself happy in my personal life, I imagine

_____ .

10. The reason I'm not as happy as I could be is _____

_____ .

11. To get more of what I want, I would have to _____

_____ .

12. To be more successful in an area that currently frustrates me, I need to change myself by _____

_____ .

13. When I think about changing myself to become more successful, I feel _____

_____ .

14. When I picture my mother, I see _____

_____ .

15. When I picture my father, I see _____

_____.

As with the checklists, you may find yourself feeling angry, anxious, sad, or defensive in response to some of the questions. That's usually a sign that something is going on, so give yourself lots of time to explore the questions that upset you most. You might talk over your feelings with a friend or, even better, write about them in a journal. Writing about your feelings gives you time to process them and put them in perspective. It's also a great way to chart your progress.

Whatever comes up as you consider these questions, take heart. There is a way to fight free of your hidden fears and get in touch with your buried dreams, and that's exactly what the rest of this book is for.

Granted, this process may take time. You may not know right away whether you really want to have a family, become a heart surgeon, move to another city, or enter a traditional marriage. You may need time to decide which compromises you're willing to make, which aspects of your dreams are truly important, and which can be left behind. Facing your fears can also take time, as well as generating pain, anger, grief, and confusion. But I believe that it's better to see yourself as a work in progress—as someone in the process of deciding and choosing—than to choose false goals and then keep yourself from getting them.

So let's keep going!

CHAPTER 2

Imagine the Life That's Right for You

Shana was a tall, rangy woman in her midtwenties, with short, dark-red hair and a dramatic manner. One day, after we'd been working together for a few months, she strode into my office, flung herself into her usual chair, and with an emphatic wave of her long arms, declared that she had received a clear message from the universe: she just wasn't meant to be a writer. She was going to give up this lifelong dream, she told me, because she had finally realized that it just wasn't in her power to make it come true.

When I questioned her about this sudden decision, I learned that Shana's novel had just been rejected by the fifth agent to whom she'd sent it. "Obviously, my work is just no good," Shana said earnestly. "I get it, I can take it. I'll just have to find something else." Then she burst into tears.

I have several friends who are writers, so I knew that five agent rejections, while admittedly painful, is nothing out of the ordinary. Indeed, I knew many people who have been rejected by ten times that many agents, editors, and publishers—and have eventually gone on to have successful writing careers. So I asked Shana to tell me more about what her expectations had been. It turned out that a woman Shana had gone to college with—"Two years behind me!" Shana pointed out—had just had her first novel published, to great acclaim. In Shana's view, that classmate's success was proof of her own failure—indeed, it was proof that Shana would never succeed.

Shana's writing meant a great deal to her, and her tears at the thought of abandoning it were heartfelt. But she honestly believed that not having succeeded yet was a solid indication that she'd never be able to succeed. Instead of envisioning the life she wanted and then taking a realistic look at what might be required to get it, Shana felt that life itself should show her the way. And she imagined that any difficulty, setback, or pain she encountered was a sign from life that she wasn't meant to be on her current path. Success, Shana believed, should come quickly and easily, and if it didn't, she should switch paths and try something else.

Despite Shana's youth and inexperience, I was struck by her assumptions, because on some level they're typical of so many people I know, both as patients and in my daily life. Often people don't realize how hard most successful people have worked to achieve their success, whether in marriage, parenthood, career, friendships, financial stability, or some other domain. We all tend to fall prey to "the grass is always greener" syndrome, idealizing the people we know who have attained success while ignoring the crises, setbacks, uncertainty, and despair they may have experienced along the way. As a result, we give up on our own dreams far too easily. Worse, we don't do the initial work that most successful people begin with: getting in touch with what they really want and deciding, realistically, what they're willing to do to get there.

To help Shana with this process, I asked her to imagine how she'd feel if she wrote two hours a day, five days a week, for the next fifteen years. The first two novels she wrote in this way would be rejected, but her third would be published. It would sell fairly well but would not make her famous or become a best seller. What might happen after that would be open-ended. If I could guarantee her that scenario, I asked, would she still prefer to abandon her work?

Shana stared at me as though I'd begun speaking Greek. Clearly, this more measured and long-term vision of her future had never occurred to her. "I honestly don't know," she said slowly. "I'd have to think about it." But thinking about it, she realized, was a far cry from the way she'd begun the session.

Shana's problem was that she misunderstood how difficult it might be for her to achieve her own personal version of success. Other patients, such as Paul, had to redefine their notions of success in ways that fit them better. Instead of picking a ready-made version of success that wasn't right for him, Paul had to uncover his buried dreams and craft a vision for a life that would truly satisfy him.

My patient Ronnie had a third problem. She knew what she wanted—marriage and a family—but she had trouble connecting wholeheartedly to her passion for that life. She came to see me, week after week, miserable because she was in her midthirties and not yet married, worried that soon she'd be too old to have children. Yet when I asked her to describe the marriage she envisioned or to talk about what she found appealing in the prospect of raising small children, she grew vague, almost uncomfortable.

"I just know I'll be miserable if I don't get it, all right?" she said to me angrily one day. "I don't want to think about why I want it or what else might make me happy—it's too upsetting. I just want you to tell me how to get what I want."

Ronnie, it seemed to me, was stuck in a kind of halfway place. She seemed to find it too painful to connect to her supposed desire for marriage and a family. But she also refused to consider the possibility that perhaps she really wanted something else, a more independent life, or perhaps a partnership without children. By not opening herself to her true passions and desires, Ronnie had gotten herself stuck in a holding position. She couldn't access the energy that passion and commitment can bring—nor could she open up to the possibility that perhaps her true passions lay elsewhere.

I agree with those who insist that success is not a destination but a journey. Sometimes we need to set ourselves a goal and pursue it with all our might. Sometimes, though, we need to be ready to catch the curveballs life throws at us, to revise our goals and dreams in the service of new ones that fit us better, to take advantage of surprising new opportunities we never even considered. And through it all, we need to remember these words of Albert Schweitzer: "Success is not the key to happiness. Happiness is the key to success. If you love what you are doing, you will be successful." Often, though, finding what you love and putting yourself in the position to doing it—whether what you're doing is writing a novel, falling in love, or raising children—is a long and complicated journey with many ups and downs.

What I've learned—in both my practice and my life—is that it's crucial to define that journey and its goals in ways that fit your personality, your passion, and your values. You need to become aware of the fears and anxieties that interfere with accessing your true desires, and you need to focus on what you really want, not what you think you should want. Only in that way can you allow yourself to feel how deeply you want your own version of success—a depth of feeling you need to fuel your journey.

Before you begin the exercises in the rest of this chapter, I'd like you to consider three questions, all of which are key to imagining a life that's right for you:

1. What do I really want?

2. What's required to get it?

3. Do I want it enough to do what's required?

I can't stress the next point too strongly: there is no right answer to that last question. In fact, realizing that you don't want something enough to pay the price for it can be a tremendously liberating experience that frees you to choose another dream, another goal, another journey.

So let's get started! The following exercises offer you a variety of approaches to imagining a life that is right for you. You can do them all, in order; skip around; or just complete the ones that appeal to you. Whatever you do, follow your own instincts—there's no better way to access the passion, commitment, and endurance you will need to make your dreams come true.

Imagine What You Really Want

To learn more about what you really want, complete the following questionnaire. Rather than laboring over each question, try to write down the first thing that comes to your mind, even if—*especially* if—it seems silly or unrealistic. Remember, the goal is to uncover your dreams.

QUESTIONNAIRE
Am I Pursuing Goals
That I Truly Desire?

Career/Life's Work

1. In the next five years, I'd like to _____

    _____.

2. In the next ten years, I'd like to _____

    _____.

3. In the next twenty years, I'd like to _____

    _____.

4. List three obstacles that you believe are keeping you from getting as much career satisfaction as you would like:

     a. _____

     b. _____

     c. _____

5. What do you think you could do to minimize, eliminate, or endure those obstacles more effectively? _____

_____.

Reread the answers to the previous five questions.

6. What's the first thought that comes to mind? _____

_____.

7. Physically, how are you feeling right now

     In your chest? _____.

     In your stomach? _____.

     In your throat? _____.

     In your forehead? _____.

     Elsewhere? _____.

     Overall? _____.

8. What's going on emotionally? Are you feeling

     Sad? _____.

     Angry? _____.

     Scared? _____.

     Happy? _____.

     Other? _____.

9. If you were given a guaranteed income and access to any entry-level position you chose, what would you do for the next five years? _____

_____.

10. What would you do for the ten years after that? _____
   _____.

11. What would you do for the rest of your life? _____
   _____.

12. How does what you just imagined compare to what you actually expect to be doing? _____
   _____.

13. How do you feel about the answer you just wrote? _____
   _____.

14. Check in with yourself physically once again. What do you notice about how you're feeling? _____
   _____.

15. Think for a moment about how your ideal career and your actual career compare. What do you think about the similarities or differences between them? Does it make you want to revise your ideal, change your actual situation, or perhaps both? Or would you say you're relatively satisfied with the path your career is taking and comfortable with the idea of continuing pretty much as you have been? _____
   _____.

Write in your journal for five minutes—more if you like—about what you've learned, felt, or decided based on the previous exercise. Or just pick up your pen and begin to write—see what flows without your overly thinking about it or controlling it.

Love Life/Personal Life

1. In the next five years, I'd like to _____
   _____.

2. In the next ten years, I'd like to _____
   _____.

3. In the next twenty years, I'd like to _____
   _____.

4. List three obstacles that you believe are keeping you from getting as much personal satisfaction as you would like:

   a. _____

   b. _____

   c. _____

5. What do you think you could do to minimize, eliminate, or endure those obstacles more effectively? _____
   _____.

Reread the answers to the previous five questions.

6. What's the first thought that comes to mind? _____
   _____.

7. Physically, how are you feeling right now

   In your chest? _____.

   In your stomach? _____.

   In your throat? _____.

   In your forehead? _____.

   Elsewhere? _____.

   Overall? _____.

8. What's going on emotionally? Are you feeling

   Sad? _____.

   Angry? _____.

   Scared? _____.

Happy? _____.

Other? _____.

9. If you were given the power to create the perfect personal life for yourself—ideal in terms of love, romance, family, friends, and activities—what would you do for the next five years?

   _____

   _____.

10. What would you do for the ten years after that? _____

    _____.

11. What would you do for the rest of your life? _____

    _____.

12. How does what you just imagined compare to what you actually expect to be doing? _____

    _____.

13. How do you feel about the answer you just wrote? _____

    _____.

14. Check in with yourself physically once again. What do you notice about how you're feeling? _____

    _____.

15. Think for a moment about how your ideal personal life and your actual personal life compare. What do you think about the similarities or differences between them? Does it make you want to revise your ideal, change your actual situation, or perhaps both? Or would you say you're relatively satisfied with the path your personal life is taking and comfortable with the idea of continuing pretty much as you have been? _____

    _____.

Write in your journal for five minutes—more if you like—about what you've learned, felt, or decided based on the previous exercise. Or just pick up your pen and begin to write—see what flows without your overly thinking about it or controlling it.

Check In with Yourself

How are you feeling right now? Often, with exercises like these, people respond by feeling angry, anxious, sad, or defensive in response to some of the questions. As we saw before, such responses often indicate that you've hit a nerve, an area in your life that needs more attention. Give yourself plenty of time to figure out these issues at your own pace, using your journal or a loved one to help you process your emotions. If you continue to feel disturbed by these issues after a day or two, I invite you to consider a response such as yoga, meditation, tai chi, or one of the martial arts, all of which are excellent ways to get in touch with your deepest self while releasing anxiety and gaining clarity. A therapist, counselor, or support group also can be extremely helpful as you come to terms with these issues.

Visualize What You Really Want

You might find it helpful to make tapes of the following visualization exercise, as well as others throughout this book, so you can listen to the tape while allowing your mind to roam free. You also can ask a friend or your spouse to read the exercise aloud—or just read it to yourself, silently. Experiment to find which is the most effective way of letting your mind travel to thoughts, images, and responses that may surprise you.

EXERCISE
Visualize Your Life's Path

1. *Relax.* As always, close your eyes and begin with a few moments of deep breathing. Shift your focus by keying in to your body, starting with the crown of your head and moving your awareness down slowly past your scalp, forehead, eyes, face, throat, arms, hands, and fingers; down your chest, torso, stomach, and groin; down your hips, thighs, knees, legs, and toes. Instruct your awareness to remain in touch with your entire physical self, and to notice how you feel physically as you proceed through this exercise.

2. *See yourself on your life path.* Imagine yourself walking down your life path. Let yourself picture this path however seems right to you—a beaten track in a meadow, a trail in a forest, a busy city street, a quiet road through a town. See yourself walking down the path. Take some time to appreciate the pleasure of moving through your world, noticing whatever sights, smells, sounds, and sensations come your way.

3. *Visit a place that holds a clue to your journey.* Now you are about to visit a place that holds an important clue to your life path. Someone you meet at that place will reveal key information to you about where you need to go on your life journey and what you need to get there. Imagine stopping at this place. What does it look like? What do you see, hear, smell, feel? Whom do you meet there? Someone you know? A stranger? A magical figure? An animal? What advice do you get?

4. *Receive a gift.* Whomever you've met at this place gives you a gift to take with you—a gift that will help you on your journey. What do you receive? Look at it closely. Again, take it in with all your senses—sight, hearing, smell, taste, touch.

5. *Imagine how you'll use the gift*. As you express your appreciation for what you've received, tell whoever gave it to you how you plan to use it and how it will help you.

6. *Continue on your journey*. Return to the path you've chosen for your journey. Has it changed at all since you were on it before? Notice as much as you can about your path and your own experience of being on it.

7. *Return to your current surroundings*. Allow yourself to leave the life path you've imagined to return to the place where you're sitting. Before you go, remind yourself that this place will always be here for you and that you can return to it whenever you wish. Create a gentle transition by leaving your eyes closed and returning your awareness to your body. Check in with yourself once again, this time beginning with your toes, and moving up to your shins, calves, thighs, and hips; from your fingertips up your arms, elbows, and shoulders; from your groin up to your stomach, torso, chest, throat, face, eyes, forehead, and scalp, coming to rest finally at the crown of your head. Take a moment to feel the connection between your crown and the world around you. Breathe deeply for a few moments, leaving your awareness there. Then open your eyes.

8. *Write about your experience*. It's key to process the experience you've had in writing, so that you can consolidate your memories by translating your feelings from emotions into words. Write for at least five minutes—more if you like—describing what you've learned, how you feel, and what you plan to do next.

9. *Involve your dream life*. If you like, as you're falling asleep tonight, instruct yourself to dream about what happened and what you learned. Your unconscious may contribute additional symbols and clues to help you get in touch with your deepest wishes.

10. *Write about what you've dreamed*. As always, give form and structure to your experience by writing about it. Keep a jour-

nal near your bed, and when you wake up, take a few minutes to jot down what you dreamed and how you feel about it.

EXERCISE
Visualize Your Life's Goal

1. *Relax.* Here's another way to achieve relaxation. Picture a flight of eighteen stairs, either at a place you know or at one you imagine—at a castle, perhaps. At the foot of the stairs is a beautiful room with a writing desk. Close your eyes and imagine yourself at the top of the stairs. Take in a full breath and let it out slowly. Now imagine yourself taking your first step down the stairs. Note this stair as number eighteen and take another breath. Take another step, counting stair number seventeen as you take another breath. Continue descending, breathing, and counting backward until you have reached step number one at the bottom of the stairs. Then enter the safe and beautiful room you have imagined.

2. *Prepare to imagine writing.* See yourself sitting at the writing desk you have imagined. Take a moment to savor the comfortable chair, the beautiful desk, the magnificent pen. Imagine yourself pulling open the desk drawer to discover a stack of writing paper and some envelopes. See yourself taking out a single page and an envelope. Then close the drawer.

3. *Imagine writing yourself a message.* See yourself picking up the pen and writing yourself a message on the paper. The message might be your life goal itself, or it might be something important you need to know to achieve that goal. See yourself writing and imagine reading the words you have written. Pay careful attention to the message you are sending yourself.

4. *Preserve your message.* When you have finished "writing," see yourself folding up the page and putting it into the envelope.

Seal the envelope and put it into the drawer. Then take another blank page from the drawer and place it on the desk. Remind yourself that the next page will be there waiting for you whenever you want to return.

5. *Return to your current surroundings.* See yourself standing up, pushing the chair back to its original place, and walking back to the flight of eighteen stairs. Begin to climb the stairs, pausing at each one to count and take a deep breath. This time count upward, with step number one being the first stair, breathing and counting at each step until you have reached step number eighteen. Notice that the higher you go, the more alert you become. When you reach the top of the stairs, notice that you are fully alert. Remain with your eyes closed for one more breath, taking pleasure in what you have accomplished.

6. *Write about what you've accomplished.* Preserve your message to yourself by writing it in your journal, along with any other thoughts and feelings that come to mind.

Access Your Passion

Once you've uncovered your dreams, you may need some extra energy to pursue them. The following exercise can help you access your passion to fuel your journey.

EXERCISE
Invite Your Passion
to Fuel Your Journey

1. *Relax.* Again, close your eyes and breathe deeply. Your goal is to open yourself completely to yourself, to remove all tension

and any obstacles that are blocking your access to your passion. If you find it helpful, see yourself descending the flight of eighteen stairs to a safe and beautiful place.

2. *Check in with your body.* Starting with the crown of your head, move your awareness inch by inch all the way down to your toes. As your awareness travels, invite each part of your body to open up and become energized.

3. *Visualize your body.* In your mind's eye, see the energy that emanates from your body. Allow yourself to visualize this energy as specifically as you can. Perhaps you're seeing one solid energy field that surrounds all of you; perhaps there are gaps and bulges in certain areas; perhaps there are different-colored or different-textured energies in different places; and so on. Allow yourself to get a picture of yourself and your energy as you are right now.

4. *Think of a goal you're deeply committed to.* Then ask yourself where the passion for that goal lives. Visualize the part of your body that holds this passion: Your stomach? Your heart? Your lungs? Your forehead? Your throat? Some other place? See what images come to mind or what words flow into your head when you ask yourself where the greatest energy and drive to fulfill this desire might live.

5. *Place your hands where that energy lives.* Gently place your hands, palm down, side by side if possible, on the home of your passion and energy for the goal you've identified. See if you can feel that energy and warmth in your palms. As you put your hands in place, tell yourself that you are inviting your passion to emerge and grow stronger, so it can help energize you for the journey ahead. See your passion intensify as your hands remain in place.

6. *Release your energy.* After about five minutes, thank your energy for responding and gently remove your hands. Remain in place, breathing deeply, for a few minutes. Then slowly

return your awareness to your body, working your way up from your toes to the crown of your head. Open your eyes.

7. *Write about your experience.* As you write in your journal, ask yourself as well what else you can do to access your passion for achieving your life goals.

Uncovering Dreams, Discovering Fears

In part one, you've had a chance to think more clearly, deeply, and openly about the life you really want. But uncovering the dreams and desires that you may have buried is only the first step toward getting the life you really want. The next step is to identify hidden fears that may be getting in your way. To learn more about the fears that may have been driving you to sabotage your own progress, keeping you from the life you want, move on to part two.

PART TWO

Identify Your Hidden Fears

Three Big Fears: Failure, Mediocrity, and Success

My patient Gloria was confused. A thin, intense woman in her early forties with short, beautifully coiffed ash-blond hair, she had come to me because, as she put it, "I feel so driven! I can never let down and just relax." A self-described workaholic, Gloria put in long hours at her job as an administrator with a major dance company. She somehow found time to work out regularly with a personal trainer. She always looked perfectly turned out, so clearly she gave her wardrobe and makeup a lot of attention as well. After a bitter divorce about five years ago, she had fallen in love with a new man, Nick, who seemed completely devoted to her and whom she loved deeply in return.

When Gloria finished describing this apparently perfect life, I asked her what I ask all my patients: "How can I help?"

Gloria frowned. "I have this fabulous life—but I can't enjoy any of it. I keep feeling that it's all going to vanish, that somehow

I've made it all up. 'Nick is going to leave me, my boss is going to fire me, I never was any good at anything'—you know." She brushed an invisible thread from her long silk skirt. "I feel like I have to work so hard at all of it. Is life really supposed to be this hard?" She tried to laugh as she concluded, "And I have to be so perfect all the time. I guess I have a terrible fear of failure."

"That's one way of looking at it," I said when she fell silent. "But in my view, most people who fear failure haven't gone after difficult professional goals the way you have. They don't bounce back from a difficult divorce the way you have, either. People who fear failure would often prefer to do nothing rather than risk doing it badly."

"Well, that's certainly not me," Gloria said drily. "Once I make up my mind, I'll do anything—and I'll keep doing it until I'm perfect at it. Hey, if you've got a brick wall you'd like me to put my head through, just let me know. Eventually I'll do it brilliantly."

"So," I said, "did it ever occur to you that maybe what you have is not a fear of failure but a fear of mediocrity?"

Gloria's jaw dropped. "I never thought of it that way," she said slowly. "But yes. That's exactly what I have."

Like many people I meet—as patients, professionally, and socially—Gloria had confused the different fears we might have regarding failure, mediocrity, and success. Too often, when we start to become aware of our hidden fears and mixed emotions, we mislabel the dynamics we're just beginning to know. One common mistake is to lump together fear of failure, fear of mediocrity, and fear of success, labeling them all as fear of failure. But the distinction is crucial, so let me make it clear:

- *Fear of failure is a dread of not succeeding.* It often leads you to avoid risks and pull back from any occasion in which you might fail.

- *Fear of mediocrity is a terror of not succeeding at the level you want to.* It often drives you to work hard—sometimes excessively—to avoid mediocrity and achieve excellence.

- *Fear of success is an anxiety about the consequences that you believe success will bring, such as envy, isolation, guilt, anger, not being a real man or a real woman, or being trapped in a "dream life" that you don't really want.* It often leads you to "drive with the emergency brake on": working hard on the one hand and sabotaging your own efforts on the other, usually without even being aware that you're in conflict.

Now that we've defined these hidden fears, let's take a closer look at each of them. You may discover that you suffer from one, two, or all three, and you also may recognize them in people you know. These aren't hard-and-fast categories—all of us are likely to feel each of these fears at least once in our lives. The question is not whether you've ever experienced a particular fear but whether a hidden form of it has come to dominate your life.

Are You Driven by Fear of Failure?

If you're driven by fear of failure, you may feel that nothing seems worse than the humiliation of not doing well. Perhaps you'd even prefer to end up with nothing—no satisfying relationship, no fulfilling job, no happy personal life—rather than risk looking foolish, wrong, or incapable. Getting the life you want seems less important than avoiding the failure you fear.

Suppose you're driven by fear of failure and you attend a party. You want to meet a desirable man, but you're afraid you're not pretty or interesting enough to attract anyone. You worry that if you approach a man who finds you unattractive, you'll be humiliated—and the shame seems unbearable. You genuinely want to meet someone, but your hidden fear of failure outweighs your deep desire for love. In fact, you're so afraid of failing that you might well spend the whole evening without talking to anyone. Even if an attractive man speaks to you, you might cut the conversation short rather than risk the failure you're sure will follow.

And if you do somehow enter a conversation, you may find subtle ways of indicating that you're not really good enough—and you know it. In effect, you'll avoid failure—in the form of rejection—by rejecting yourself first.

Fear of failure may extend to every area of your life: love, work, friendship, family. Or it may center on one or two areas—you may be a risk-taker in love, for example, who backs off when it comes to career, or perhaps you're a brave striver in the work world who fears failure in romance. Either way, fear of failure can be a powerful brake that prevents you from pursuing your quest for the life you really want.

How Fear of Failure Can Hold You Back

Ironically, the more you fear failure, the more likely you are to fail. In fact, telling yourself to avoid failure seems to create a nearly irresistible compulsion to fail!

Sometimes that compulsion is caused by anxiety: you worry so much about failing that it may seem easier just to fail and get it over with. You might tell yourself, "Since I'm so sure that guy will reject me sooner or later, I'll make sure it happens sooner so I don't have to keep worrying about it." Sometimes your failure is a result of the ironic processes we explored in chapter 1: telling yourself not to do something inspires your Monitor to look for all the evidence that you are doing it, evidence that can sometimes feel overwhelming.

An interesting study conducted with soldiers in the Israeli Army demonstrates how fearing failure often makes failure seem inevitable—even when you're actually capable of succeeding. Researcher Shlomo Breznitz knew that Israeli soldiers are routinely woken in the middle of the night and told to run four miles wearing a heavy pack. This is a standard aspect of Israeli military training, and eventually, every soldier learns to do it.

But when Dr. Breznitz had soldiers woken in the night and asked to run ten miles, many soldiers became overwhelmed at the mere idea of this daunting task. As a result, a significant number of them stopped running not just before they had achieved ten miles, but before they had achieved four. Clearly, had the researchers asked the soldiers to run four miles, they'd have had no problem succeeding. But by asking them to run ten, he tapped into some soldiers' fear of failure, and as a result, they couldn't even run as far as they'd already proven they could.

Dr. Breznitz doesn't go into detail about how this self-sabotage occurred, but my own theory is that ironic processes just took over. Wishing to avoid failure, the soldiers began unconsciously to look for every possible indication that they would fail—every sign of fatigue, discomfort, incapacity. Finally, overwhelmed by this mounting evidence of failure, they simply gave up.

Another possible explanation is that the fear of failure raised the soldiers' anxiety to intolerable levels—and that anxiety had a disabling effect. As we know, stress is a biological phenomenon that can sometimes inspire you to great feats—the famous "fight or flight" mechanism. But while a certain degree of stress can invigorate you, inspiring you to try harder and achieve more, too much stress can have the opposite effect. Overwhelmed, you simply give up and shut down.

That's why people driven by fear of failure tend to do worse in school and on the job. When you feel stress, your brain releases a set of hormones known as glucocorticoids. These potent chemicals destroy other neurons in your brain and reduce optimal functioning of your hippocampus, the center for long-term memory. (If you saw the film *Memento*, you'll recall that the memory-impaired main character had a damaged hippocampus.) So in a very real way, feeling stressed and anxious can keep you from remembering what you've learned. Stress also can interfere with your ability to think clearly and to rationally assess a situation.

Maybe that's why a provocative 2003 research report conducted in Sweden indicates that failure is associated with increased risk of school injuries, dropping out of school, violence, depression, and suicide attempts. According to the report, as children fail in school, they become discouraged, depressed, and more likely to drop out. Dropping out of school engenders other social problems, and a pattern of failure is set, with each component making the others worse.

A pair of Australian researchers, Andrew J. Martin and Herbert W. Marsh, shed further light in their own study of students and failure. They suggest that many people who fear failure are actually more concerned with avoiding the implications of failure. Such people fear that failing would reveal some terrible truth about them—and they'll do anything to avoid confronting that fear.

Sometimes people avoid confronting their fears through a strategy that the researchers labeled *self-handicapping*: deliberately (unconsciously) creating obstacles that can be blamed for their failure. A self-handicapping student, for example, might avoid studying for a test. Then, when he fails, he can blame his F on the fact that he didn't study. It's simply too upsetting to him to consider the possibility that he could have studied his hardest—and still failed.

Adults use this strategy, too. For example, a self-handicapping woman who feared failure in dating might deliberately dress in a sloppy or unattractive manner, telling herself she "doesn't have time" to fix herself up. Then, when she doesn't get a date, she can blame it on her unattractive appearance, secretly knowing that she didn't really give herself her best shot. By purposely (unconsciously) setting herself up for failure, she leaves herself a tiny margin of hope—and avoids confronting her worst fears.

The researchers also talk about "defensive pessimism": setting unrealistically low expectations. That way you steel yourself against failure—and lower your standards. The student who insists he'll get a D on the test won't be disappointed if that's the grade he gets, and he might actually be happy to get a C-minus. Had he expected a higher grade and not gotten it, the apparent failure would flood him with feelings of self-doubt and self-hatred. Lower expectations keep him from confronting his worst fears, at the cost of a very low opinion of himself.

Likewise, a woman who insists that no good man could ever care for her or that she isn't smart enough to succeed at a demanding job may be trying to protect herself from her fear of failure. To her and others driven by this fear, the fear of failure is far more powerful than the lure of success.

This mind-set quickly produces a vicious cycle: the more you fear failure, the more anxious you become; the more anxious you feel, the more likely you are to fail; the more often you fail, the more justified your fear seems to be. Approaching men in a timid, self-defeating way, you're more likely to get a negative response—proving that no good man will ever look at you. Accepting a new promotion, you're too anxious to take charge properly and too stressed out to think clearly. Like the Israeli soldiers, you're so overwhelmed by fear, you can't even do as well as you did before, let alone rise to the new challenge. Paralyzed by your fears, you fail—and withdraw further to avoid future failures.

Where does fear of failure come from? According to researchers Andrew Elliot and Todd Thrash, we're more likely to be driven by this fear if our parents were, particularly since mothers who fear failure are more likely than other mothers to withdraw their love when their child fails. Researcher Richard Teevan found that children with a high fear of failure tended to have mothers who punished them for failing, but who reacted neutrally to success. And psychologist Wendell Smith conducted a study finding that boys who had a high fear of failure had mothers who set high standards for achievement but who didn't believe that their sons would be able to meet those standards. Presumably those findings would apply to girls and fathers as well. In other words, people whose parents punished them for failing often go on to be more committed to avoiding failure than to pursuing success. Fear of failure became the fear that dominates their lives.

Of course, no one likes to fail, and in that sense, maybe all of us are afraid of failure, at least some of the time. Certainly it's rational to avoid doing something if we think the consequences of failure will be too great. At the most primitive level, fear of failure could keep us from rushing to an untimely death: fearing failure at rock climbing, downhill skiing, or long-distance swimming, the inexperienced athlete will avoid a dangerous sport or at least start slowly. Fear of failure might keep us from making risky investments in the stock market, or embarking on a career we don't have the aptitude for, or getting involved with that charming but flighty boyfriend who isn't really available. Sure, we dream of getting rich or being famous or running off to Spain with a fabulous lover, but our fear of failure keeps us from pursuing goals that we have little chance of achieving.

Fear of failure can also keep us from hurting others: the untrained surgeon won't perform a risky procedure that she isn't capable of; the inexperienced lawyer won't take on a trial that's beyond her abilities. Knowing our abilities and our limits, we can use fear of failure to help us make good decisions about what we're capable of and what is truly beyond us.

I'm not talking about simply fearing failure—we all do that, to some extent. I'm talking about being driven by that fear, organizing your life in such a way that avoiding failure becomes your main concern. Yet you're not really aware of how this fear affects your life. You aren't saying, "I'm so devastated by even the thought of failing that I'm not even going to try." You're saying, "Hey, that guy wouldn't have looked at me anyway," or "I'm just not smart enough to get that promotion," or (in the case of the Israeli soldiers) "I'm not strong enough to run ten miles." Thus fear of failure often leads you to make dishonest or inaccurate judgments about yourself, preventing you from seeing clearly who you are and what life might hold for you.

Are You Struggling with Fear of Failure?

Is your life overly constrained by fear of failure? Is fear of failure—in one or more areas of your life—preventing you from trying new things? Would you rather avoid a relationship than risk the possibility of it not working out? Are you working below your capacity to ensure that you'll never fail? Is fear of failure preventing you from getting the life you really want?

To help yourself answer these questions, look at the following checklist. Does any of these items ring a bell with you? If it does, put a check mark in the appropriate box.

CHECKLIST
Am I Held Back by Fear of Failure?

☐   I avoid doing any activity I don't think I'll be good at.

☐   If I start an activity and discover it doesn't come easily to me, I find a reason to stop.

☐   It's been years since I took a class, started a new activity, or learned anything new.

☐   All things being equal, I prefer not to meet new people.

☐   I often worry that I won't be liked or that I'll make a poor impression.

☐   I have stayed away from career opportunities because I didn't think I could handle them.

☐   I avoid pursuing as romantic partners or friends people I think are out of my league.

☐   I often feel that people expect more from me than I can reasonably be expected to produce.

☐ The very thought of trying something new makes me nervous.

☐ I would rather give in than stand my ground in a disagreement—even when I know I'm right.

☐ I often find myself giving in to my romantic partner, family, or friends, just to keep the peace.

☐ I'm happiest when I'm out of the spotlight.

☐ If I can't do something well after two or three tries, I move on to something else.

☐ When I don't understand something, I get frustrated and move on.

☐ Security is very important to me.

☐ I tend to steel myself against failure by taking a pessimistic view.

☐ I'd rather aim low and be happily surprised than aim high and be disappointed.

☐ My sense is that anything that doesn't work out is probably not meant to be.

☐ I often have trouble looking my best for dates, key business meetings, or other important occasions.

☐ I often find myself running late for my most important appointments.

☐ I have a hard time bouncing back from disappointment, especially when I think it was my fault.

If even one or two of these items seemed to describe how you feel, or if you have an intuitive sense that fear of failure plays a key role in your life, complete the following exercise for a closer look.

Get to Know Your Fear of Failure

1. *Relax.* This exercise works best if you're in a calm, relaxed frame of mind, so, as before, picture a flight of eighteen stairs, either at a place you know or at one you imagine. At the foot of the stairs is a safe and beautiful place: a comfortable room, a peaceful lake shore, or some other space that makes you feel safe and happy. Close your eyes and imagine yourself at the top of the stairs, taking and releasing a deep breath. Continue down each step, breathing at every step and counting backward from eighteen until you have reached the safe and beautiful place at the foot of the stairs.

2. *Focus on the item or items that provoked the most anxiety.* Think of the item on the fear of failure checklist that made you feel most anxious, and allow your mind to dwell on it. Keep breathing as you ask yourself to just sit with the anxiety and get to know it a bit better. Whose faces come to mind: Family members? A boss? A colleague? A spouse? Is there a particular setting that you find yourself visualizing? A time in your life? An incident from the recent or long-distant past? What people, places, or incidents do you associate with this anxiety?

3. *Ask yourself "What am I most afraid of?" and visualize the answer.* Allow your image of the anxiety-provoking situation to play itself out. For example, if you feel anxious about a work situation, see yourself doing the thing you're afraid to do and then visualize the worst possible outcome. Perhaps you're at a meeting and everyone is pointing at you and laughing. Perhaps you approach a man at a party and he says, "You're just disgusting. Get away from me." Visualize the failure you've been trying to avoid. And keep breathing. I know this may be an unpleasant experience, but try to see it through.

4. *Return to your current surroundings.* Visualize yourself climbing back up those eighteen stairs, pausing at each one to take and release a deep breath. Count each stair as you breathe, starting from one and moving up to eighteen, remaining relaxed as you breathe and count.

5. *Write down what you've imagined.* This step is extremely important, so please don't neglect it. Write down the scene you've imagined—the terrible outcome that you've always feared. Don't just jot a few notes; put your thoughts into sentences. Research has shown that people who write about traumatic events are able to recover from them more readily than people who simply talk about them or dwell on them in their thoughts. Something about writing down the trauma—whether real or imaginary—gives it a form that allows you some distance and, hopefully, some perspective. So describe in writing the failure you've envisioned. Try to include the most upsetting and painful details. Writing them down will be an important aspect of releasing them.

At this point you have three choices. You can do one, two, or all three.

1. *Rip up the page you've just written while visualizing a different outcome.* As you physically destroy your written account, visualize the same situation—without the terrible failure. Instead of everyone pointing at you and laughing, perhaps they simply shrug and look away. Instead of the man insulting you, perhaps he simply smiles and shakes his head. You can visualize a completely positive outcome—a terrific meeting, a new romance—or you can visualize a more gentle version of the failure you'd previously imagined. Either way, you're reminding yourself that you're in control of these images. You can replace an extreme fear with a more acceptable outcome anytime you want to.

2. *Turn the horrible outcome into a comic one.* This is another way of giving yourself power over your fear: exaggerate it until it becomes absurd. The laughing people at your meeting suddenly take wing and turn into cartoon Tweety birds. The rejecting man suddenly finds himself naked. You can go on to practice reenvisioning your worst fears until they become funny, harmless, or a satisfying reminder that you're not the only person in the world who fears humiliation.

3. *Continue to write—then or later—about previous times you've felt this fear, and to record your associations with it.* Does this exercise trigger a host of memories about your family? Does it bring up a series of complaints against a colleague, friend, or spouse? Does it engender a flood of tears, or a wish to yell back at someone who once made you feel small? Whatever you feel, however you react, keep writing. You don't want all these feelings to build up with no outlet. Again, writing gives your feelings a form that enables you to release them. You may return to explore these feelings once, twice, or several times, but don't just sit there and remember; put your thoughts, feelings, and images onto the page.

SCIENCE MATTERS

Revisiting Memories Can Actually Change Them

Visualizing is a powerful tool because it brings up so many emotions—emotions that are often consciously or unconsciously attached to painful memories. Fascinating new research in memory suggests that every time we revisit a memory, we have the opportunity to alter it. That's why writing about an experience is so important: it can transform the way we've processed a traumatic event, helping us come to terms with it and move on.

How does this work? Scientists now understand that re-membering something is not a fixed process, like putting away a snapshot for future reference. Instead, we create our memories as we store them in a process known as *consolidation*. Researchers now understand that whenever we return to a stored memory, we reactivate it—and then we have to reconsolidate it to store it again.

Now, here's where it gets interesting: Every time we reactivate a memory, it becomes fluid (the scientific term is labile) and susceptible to change. In a sense, we're no longer remembering the actual event; instead, we recall our memory of the event. That's why our memories are so often faulty: once we get an idea into our heads, we remember the idea, whether or not it ever happened. Each time we revisit that memory, we reactivate that idea and then reconsolidate it, perhaps changing it a bit each time. That's why past triumphs often grow sweeter as they recede farther into the past, while past failures may become more painful—or less. Our ideas about what happened can alter both our memories and the emotional charge they carry.

We'll look more closely at memory and emotion in chapter 10. Meanwhile, you can see why writing is such an important tool in overcoming the pain of past memories. Writing about your memories from your current vantage point can help you replace your past view ("That was totally humiliating, and I never want to go through that again") with a more current one ("Actually, I survived that bad experience, and I'm willing to take some new risks now"). Your journal can literally give you a chance to rewrite your memories, erasing some of the hurt and anger you once felt as you move on to acceptance and hope.

Some More Ways to Release Your Fear of Failure

- *With or without the previous exercise, keep a journal.* Write regularly about your fears, or write in your journal whenever they come up.

- *Involve a friend.* When you find yourself feeling fearful about failing, contact a friend who's agreed to be on call. Have her coach you back into the game. Make sure she knows that you want her to encourage you to take that risk, not to support you in your withdrawal.

- *Meditate or engage in yoga, tai chi, martial arts, or some other form of mind-body practice.* Studies have shown that these activities can increase relaxation, decrease stress, and increase a sense of well-being and self-esteem—important resources in your efforts to put fear in its place.

- *Challenge yourself to face your fears.* Try to do at least one thing that scares you regularly—say, once a week. Learning that you can face your fear and survive, even if you fail, may make you feel stronger.

- *Involve your dreams.* Before you fall asleep, give yourself the instruction to dream about your fears—and to dream a solution to them. Make sure a dream journal is easily accessible so you can write about what you dreamed as soon as you wake. Again, writing is extremely important; otherwise you may simply feel overwhelmed with the painful emotions from the dreams.

- *Consider therapy.* If you discover that your fears are more than you can manage by yourself, consider finding a therapist, counselor, or therapy group that can help make your progress easier.

Are You Driven by Fear of Mediocrity?

If fear of mediocrity is your driving force, you may think that the worst thing you could do would be to give up before you've reached perfection, because that would feel like accepting mediocrity. Like Gloria, you're committed to doing everything super-well—but like her, you may also feel that whatever you do is never good enough. Fearing mediocrity, you're always ready to condemn even your best efforts, because they still haven't freed you from this terrible fear.

Let's take that example of attending a party to meet a man, only now your fear is not of failure, but of mediocrity. Desiring a relationship, you'll likely make every effort to attract someone you think you might like, either making the first move yourself or finding ways to elicit a move from someone else. Committed to getting what you want, you may well succeed—at first. But as soon as you think you're making progress, you might start to question whether this man or this relationship is really good enough. Or perhaps you'll question yourself, deciding that you're not loving enough, attractive enough, sexual enough. Demanding excellence in every area of your life, you might have trouble enjoying any relationship because of your deep-seated fear that you, your partner, or your relationship is somehow mediocre.

For some people, this fear kicks in early. They feel an initial attraction to a romance, a friend, a job, an activity, but their initial desire is almost immediately blunted by their fear. No, they decide, something's not good enough here, and they either back off or work extra hard to improve themselves, the other person, the situation, or all three.

Other people manage to establish a relationship or a career, but never relax enough to enjoy it. Successful in most people's eyes, they are failures in their own, unable to appreciate what they've achieved. Still others can enjoy their achievements for a while, but then their fear of mediocrity kicks in and they begin to undermine themselves and/or their spouses, friends, coworkers. Whatever the timing, fear of mediocrity eventually spoils much of the pleasure in love, friendship, work, or personal life.

How Fear of Mediocrity
Can Hold You Back

Remember our look at ironic processes in chapter 1? Every time you try to achieve something, your Monitor kicks in, looking for evidence that you haven't done what you're trying to do. So if you're driven by a fear of mediocrity, watch out: your Monitor will soon supply you with more than enough evidence to prove that you actually are mediocre.

As you can see, this can easily become a vicious circle: you fear mediocrity, you engage in a difficult task, you achieve something great—and your Monitor finds every possible piece of evidence that it wasn't so great after all. So you engage in an even more daunting task, pursue an even more difficult goal—you succeed—and your Monitor points out everything else in your life that needs work. Your fear of mediocrity is like a fire. You toss each new achievement in, hoping to put out the fire—but instead you've just added fuel. The more you do, the better you are, the greater your achievements, the greater your fear of mediocrity becomes, and the less certain you feel of being able to overcome it.

As a result, many people struggling with this fear feel like imposters. In fact, this response is so common that scientists have even given it a name: the Imposter Phenomenon. In a study conducted of 104 midlevel managers, researcher Sharon Fried-Buchalter discovered that people who felt like imposters experienced generalized anxiety, lack of self-confidence, frustration, and depression, because they were unable to meet their own standards. As we've just seen, they'd set themselves standards that they'd never be able to meet—by definition—so the Imposter Phenomenon had condemned them to a life of misery.

An earlier study of undergraduates, graduate students, medical students, and professional women found similar results: women who felt like imposters suffered from generalized anxiety, lack of self-confidence, frustration, and depression. Writing in

1978, the researchers also indicated that the Imposter Phenomenon was more common among women than men. Men, they suggested, tended to attribute their success to their own abilities, whereas women were more likely to give credit either to luck or to their social skills. I'm sorry to say that some thirty years later, I notice the same tendency among my patients. Men tend to assume their successes are their own doing, while women insist they "just got lucky." As a result, they feel anxious about succeeding and worry that their luck will soon run out.

Of course, men suffer from the Imposter Phenomenon as well. In fact, the problem is so common among both sexes that it was the subject of a 2005 article in the *Harvard Business Review*, "The Dangers of Feeling Like a Fake." Psychoanalyst and international business consultant Manfred F. R. Kets de Vries points out that managers who feel like imposters are likely to harm their companies by creating a workplace culture of workaholism and by exerting too much control and micromanagement.

Perfectionism comes into play here. When a perfectionist sets unrealistic goals for herself and then can't meet them, she tends to feel like an imposter. This feeling triggers a bout of self-flagellation and renewed hard work, which inspires yet another set of unattainable goals.

In my view, the vicious cycle that de Vries describes is a perfect example of how fear of mediocrity triggers the ironic process of Monitoring: your fear leads you to seek evidence that your fear is justified; and seeking it, you will always find it. It's a bit like the medieval trials that attempted to discover witches by dunking them in a pond: if you survived, you were a witch; only if you died could you be innocent. To the perfectionist who fears mediocrity, if you've got any energy left after a work session, you haven't tried hard enough. Only total exhaustion is good enough to prove you've done your best—and eventually even that isn't sufficient!

I must admit to sharing a bit of this fear myself. A few years ago, I trained diligently for the Boston Marathon, having already run four marathons in Boston and New York. In fact, I broke my own record by twenty minutes. But I'm embarrassed to admit that I wasn't satisfied with this achievement. Instead, I focused on the fact that when I crossed the finish line, I didn't collapse! "I could have worked a little harder," I said to myself. "After all, I ran my last mile in only six minutes—to run it that fast means I must have been saving up some extra energy that I actually should have spent." It took me quite some time to shift my focus, asking not "Did I exhaust myself completely?" but rather "Did I do the best I could on that particular day?" Only when I accepted that I had done my best—not some mythical best that I invented out of the blue—could I refocus my attention and appreciate my achievement.

Now, let's not forget: fear of mediocrity can also have many positive effects. It can push you to achieve the very best of which you're capable, refusing to let you settle or compromise when you don't need to. For example, fear of mediocrity gave my patient Gloria the courage to leave an unsatisfying marriage, endure a bitter divorce, and find a new love that was far more fulfilling. It propelled her to the top of a demanding, difficult, risky profession, and it helped shape her into a person of uncompromising principle and integrity. Fear of mediocrity pushed me to train hard for my fifth marathon, and to take twenty minutes off my previous best time. I encourage you, too, to think of all the ways that fear of mediocrity has been a positive force in your life.

The problem, as with fear of failure, is not in feeling this fear, but in being unaware of it. Refusing to acknowledge her hidden fear, Gloria had become unable to control it. But if she doesn't attend to this suppressed emotion, she won't be able to transform it into a positive desire for excellence. Instead of using her fear, it will use her.

So again, the real question is not whether you feel this fear, but to what extent it holds you back. Fear of mediocrity can be a powerful impetus for fulfilling your desires, but you need to know it's there and put it in perspective.

Are You Struggling with Fear of Mediocrity?

Is your life dominated by a fear of mediocrity? Look at the following checklist and see whether any items ring true. If any does, put a check mark in the appropriate box.

CHECKLIST
Am I Held Back by Fear of Mediocrity?

- ☐ If I start an activity and discover I'm not good at it, I redouble my efforts.

- ☐ If I can't be good at something after a few tries, I may find a reason to drop it.

- ☐ It's important to me to make a good impression on almost everyone.

- ☐ If I had to choose, I'd rather be respected than liked.

- ☐ If you tell me I can't do something, it's like a red flag to a bull: I have to prove you wrong.

- ☐ If a romantic partner seems uninterested or unavailable, I regard that as a positive challenge.

- ☐ In relationships, I'm almost always the one who does the breaking up; very few people have ever broken up with me.

- ☐ I can't say I've ever really failed at anything.

- ☐ Whenever I've failed, I've redoubled my efforts to succeed either in the same place or somewhere else.

- ☐ People who give up easily get on my nerves.

- ☐ I don't understand people who are satisfied with doing less than their best.

☐   I often get my way in my relationship.

☐   I often get my way at work.

☐   I'm happiest when I'm taking on a challenge.

☐   Achievement is very important to me.

☐   When I feel anxious, I tend to work harder.

☐   Although I've achieved a lot, I find it hard to relax and enjoy my accomplishments.

☐   I feel lost and anxious without a new challenge or a new project to start.

☐   My family and friends often complain about my being too busy for them.

☐   I am more comfortable being too busy than not busy enough.

☐   Whatever I do, I want to be the best.

☐   I am often dissatisfied with accomplishments that I know other people would be satisfied with.

If even one or two of these items seemed to describe how you feel, or if you have an intuitive sense that fear of mediocrity plays a key role in your life, complete the following exercise for a closer look.

EXERCISE
Get to Know Your Fear of Mediocrity

1. *Relax.* Put yourself into a calm, relaxed frame of mind by clearing your mind through visualization. As before, imagine a flight of eighteen stairs leading down to a safe and beautiful place, either one you know or one you can imagine. Close your eyes and take a deep breath. Descend the stairway, step by step, breathing at each step and counting backward from eighteen. Then enter the safe and beautiful place at the foot of the stairs, where you will remain as you complete the exercise.

2. *Focus on the item or items that provoked the most anxiety*. Let your mind center on the item on the fear of mediocrity checklist that made you feel most anxious. Continue to breathe as you ask yourself to experience the anxiety. Your goal is to pay attention to every detail of this experience, so keep your antennae up and notice as much as you can. How does your body feel? Is your chest tight? Do you feel a sinking sensation in the pit of your stomach? Where is your mind going—to a word, a phrase, an image? Do you see anyone's face? Do you hear anyone speaking to you? Does any memory float to the surface? There is no right or wrong way to do this step, so focus entirely on noticing and remembering as much as you can.

3. *Ask yourself "What am I most afraid of?" and notice what happens*. Again, there is no right or wrong way to complete this step. Your goal is not to get an answer, but to notice what happens as you ask the question. Return your attention to your physical sensations: chest, throat, forehead, the crown of your head; palms and fingers; the soles of your feet; the small of your back. Do you feel tight? Loose? Is your attention drawn to any particular place on your body? Are you seeing a color? An object? A person? A place? Notice as much as you can about your physical, mental, and emotional responses, and remember every detail. Keep breathing—that will free your attention, allowing you to notice and remember more.

4. *Return to your current surroundings*. See yourself climbing back up the flight of stairs, pausing at each one to take and release a deep breath. Count each stair as you breathe, starting from one and moving up to eighteen, remaining relaxed and alert.

5. *After five minutes have passed—more if you prefer—write down what you've noticed*. As before, this step is extremely important. Give form to your experience by putting your observations, sensations, and memories into complete sentences. Remem-

ber, research indicates that it's easier to recover from traumatic events if you write them down, because that gives them a form that enables you to release them.

6. *Repeat this exercise every day for a week.* Continue to record your experiences each day. Please, don't reread your pages; simply collect them.

7. *After a week, reread what you've written, and write your responses to what you've read.* What have you learned about how fear of mediocrity affects your life? Have you discovered more about where this fear comes from or when it's most likely to come out? Is it associated with particular times, places, people, or situations? When is it a useful force in your life, and when is it likely to hold you back? Write for at least five minutes without stopping—longer, if you prefer—in response to your rereading.

8. *Complete the following questionnaire.* I suggest answering the questions once, quickly, off the top of your head, and then again, more slowly and thoughtfully:

    a. My fear of mediocrity is most likely to emerge when

    _____
    _____.

    b. I appreciate this fear, because it has enabled me to ____

    _____.

    c. I am frustrated by this fear, because it tends to make me _____

    _____.

    d. What I would most like to do with regard to this fear is

    _____
    _____.

Some More Ways to Harness Your
Fear of Mediocrity

- *Continue to keep a journal.* Write regularly about the way your fear of mediocrity affects your life. Or turn to your journal when you feel your fear of mediocrity is interfering with your true desires—or simply with taking pleasure in your achievements.

- *Involve a friend.* When you find yourself responding to your fear of mediocrity in ways that don't work for you, get in touch with a friend. Have her suggest that you appreciate this aspect of your personality, but also put it in perspective. You might work with her to come up with a list of simple suggestions that you'll find useful in stressful times, such as taking a walk, soaking in the tub, or calling a friend to "talk you down" from your anxiety.

- *Meditate or engage in yoga, tai chi, martial arts, or some other form of mind-body practice.* These activities can be extraordinarily helpful for self-acceptance. I promise you that they'll leave your drive and ambition intact, while helping you to release your perfectionism. Make a commitment to try one of these activities for three months before evaluating how well it's worked for you. You may be surprised!

- *Practice giving yourself another focus when you feel yourself driven by fear of mediocrity.* Remember, the way to disengage your Monitor is to give your mind something else to do. You might choose a pleasant scene to visualize, keep a crossword puzzle handy, or keep a list ready of five-minute tasks that can distract your mind and give your anxiety a chance to dissipate by itself. Trying to make yourself less anxious may make you more anxious; diverting yourself with another task or interest fools your Monitor into thinking it has nothing to do.

- *Involve your dreams.* Just as you're drifting off to sleep, tell yourself that you will dream about your ideal self—the way you'd truly like to be in the world. Be aware that such dreams may be comforting, painful, or some of both, since you may end up confronting both your ideal self and the obstacles to becoming that self. Be sure to write about your dreams and the feelings they engender.

- *Consider therapy.* It can often be extremely helpful to engage in therapy, particularly if you'd like to make more progress in a shorter time. A therapist, counselor, or therapy group can give you a new perspective and perhaps some new coping techniques as well.

Are You Driven by Fear of Success?

What if your controlling fear is fear of success? In that case, it's not actually success you fear, but rather the consequences that you believe come with it—envy, isolation, guilt, anger, compromising your identity as a man or a woman, and/or being trapped in a false dream.

Fear of success is the most complicated of our three fears, because it so often disguises itself as something else. You tell yourself and everybody else what you want—and it looks like you're making every effort to get it. You may even get part of the way there. But somehow you never quite go all the way.

Why not? Well, when you fear success, you're likely to sabotage yourself, usually without even realizing it. The top athlete who suddenly falls prey to a mysterious slump, the charming woman who can never find lasting happiness with a man, the talented executive who crashes and burns at one company after another—all these people are likely suffering from a hidden fear of success, sabotaging their progress because, rightly or wrongly, they believe bad things will happen when they succeed.

Suppose that, like the women in our other examples, you're attending a party in hopes of meeting an attractive man. Perhaps, like Miriam, you're fairly certain that you can attract a man—but you're not so sure you want to. Yes, you want love. But what if bringing home a really great guy provokes the envy of your mother, your sister, your best friend? Or suppose that great guy requires you to give up your demanding career: are you ready to face that conflict? Maybe you're concerned that you will become more focused on your love life, losing your ambition and your edge; do you really want to give up the position you've worked so hard to attain?

Maybe you're wholeheartedly committed to finding love, but you're not so sure you want children. If you're not ready to confront this issue—which may bring up uncomfortable issues for you about being a woman or fulfilling your family's wishes—you might prefer to avoid the conflict by never getting involved with a marriage-minded man, even while insisting that you want to be married.

Or maybe your previous relationships haven't been all that satisfying. Maybe you're afraid that getting a guy—however great he seems at first—will only trap you once again in a painful or frustrating relationship.

For any of these reasons or perhaps some other, you may not be able to pursue a relationship wholeheartedly, since on some level you believe it will make you more unhappy, not less. In other words, you're a prisoner of your mixed emotions, fearing success even as you desire it. So rather than confronting your complicated fears and reservations, you set yourself up for failure. You want love, but you also fear it. You want to meet a guy, but you worry about what will happen once you do. And so you say you're looking for a great relationship, and part of you really is. But somehow you never meet anyone, or only the wrong guys, or else you find some way to make a good relationship fail.

As with the other fears, fear of success might characterize your entire life, or it might be limited to one or two domains. It might kick in early, keeping you at a needlessly low level of achievement, or it might appear later, coexisting with an apparently happy marriage, outstanding career, or other types of personal success. If you fear success, you might achieve the equivalent of an A, while preventing yourself from going all the way to A-plus. Or you might stop yourself at B-plus, B, or even C, depending on what you fear and how you manage it. In all of these cases, though, you're letting your hidden fears and mixed emotions keep you from the life you really want.

How Fear of Success Can Hold You Back

If you fear success—even while also desiring it—you may believe that success will provoke other people's envy, leading to isolation and the loss of cherished relationships. You might feel guilty about achieving success, fearing that others will somehow be hurt by your achievements. You could fear the anger that you believe your success will unleash, either within you or against you, or perhaps others fear that your success will somehow release their own buried anger against spouses, friends, family. They may fear that success will somehow compromise their identity as a woman or a man, or they may be concerned about a success that traps them in a false dream, one they are not ready to consciously reject but about which they have decidedly mixed emotions.

What's the solution?

1. Take another look at the checklists on pages 31–33 and 34–35 of chapter 1: "Am I Holding Myself Back without Realizing It?" and "What Do I Think about Success?"

2. If any of the items on those checklists seem true of you, make sure you've completed the questionnaire on pages 36–38 of chapter 1: "What Do You Want—and What's Holding You Back?"

3. To get an even better sense of your true desires, go on to chapter 3.

4. To learn what form of your fear of success may be taking, read the rest of the chapters in part two.

Ironically, fear of success is one of the hardest problems to overcome—in some ways, harder than fear of failure or fear of mediocrity. That's because you are divided against yourself, and you really can be your own worst enemy! But take heart. The rest of this book is devoted to helping you get in touch with your desires, identify and analyze your fears, and then decide what's really important to you.

CHAPTER 4

Overcome Your Fear of Fear Itself

As I saw it, my patient Carrie was a woman of great courage. She had endured an abusive family, a battle with addiction, and a number of other hardships on her way to earning a college degree and becoming a physical therapist. She also had worked free of several abusive romantic relationships before finally becoming involved with Joe, a faithful, loving, and hardworking man who treated her with respect. To me, it seemed that Carrie had bravely and steadfastly overcome one obstacle after another in her determined pursuit of happiness.

But Carrie saw herself as a timid, anxious person whose life was shaped by fear. Susceptible to panic attacks and prey to a host of worries, Carrie wanted to start a family but was concerned that she'd be driven to pass her own fears on to her children.

Carrie had come to me in the hope of creating a fear-free life, so she was surprised and considerably upset to hear me say one day that in my opinion, fear is a part of life—that life without fear is simply not possible.

"Then what am I doing here?" she asked, her normally quiet voice rising to a panicky squeak. "I thought getting rid of fear was what we were working on."

I asked Carrie how she would feel about accepting her fear and putting some boundaries on it, rather than expecting to eliminate it altogether. I explained that in my view, people who go on to create successful lives feel fear often—maybe even more often than those who are less successful. The people who achieve success—whether in love, work, family, or personal life—may actually be those who have best learned not how to avoid fear but to manage it. Not fear, but fear of fear, might be the problem we needed to solve.

Carrie considered this for a moment. "I guess I don't understand the difference," she said. "I hate being afraid."

"Yes," I persisted, "fear is unpleasant, and I understand why you don't like it. But rather than eliminating it altogether, can you imagine finding a way to live with your fear more comfortably than you do now?"

Carrie shook her head. "I don't know," she said. "What difference would that make? I'd still be afraid."

To help Carrie understand the distinction between fear and fear of fear, I told her about a fascinating study I'd recently read. The study concerned U.S. pilots during World War II who had been sent to Europe on daily bombing missions. Crews could expect unlimited assignments—they'd simply be sent out until eventually they'd fail to come back. Then, since the Eighth Air Force had no shortage of pilots or planes, another crew would be sent in their place.

The flight crews, who'd started their service with high morale (as it was an honor to be in one of the elite flight squadrons), soon became overwhelmed with the thought that they'd simply keep being sent out until their plane went down. They began developing the classic symptoms of war neurosis: not sleeping, not eating, becoming hysterical, responding anxiously to certain sounds, and so on. Once these symptoms appeared, they spread like wildfire among the flight crews, and many of them simply broke down and couldn't continue. (This is the situation brilliantly described by novelist Joseph Heller, himself a World War II veteran, in his classic novel *Catch-22*.)

So far, Carrie was with me, nodding emphatically. Having been through a series of seemingly endless traumas in her own life, she could well understand how unrelieved stress with no prospect of relief simply wears a person down.

The army air corps, I went on, became concerned about the drop in morale and interviewed the flight crews. The servicemen explained that they felt hopeless. They saw friends and colleagues dying all around them, and every death reminded them that they had little hope of being able to return. If they didn't die on the next flight, they'd die on the one after that, or the one after that. Every flight was viewed as a near-miss—and the situation could only get worse. In effect, they were counting an endless number of flights, with each succeeding number seen as increasing their risk of death.

So chief surgeon Dr. Malcolm C. Grow figured out a solution, and the Eighth Air Force changed its policy. They told the crews that they only had to fly twenty-five missions. Once they had survived those missions, they were home free.

Morale improved immediately, and the incidence of the stress symptoms significantly decreased. Subsequent interviews revealed that now the pilots were starting to count down toward safety instead of up toward eventual death. Rather than saying "I have an unlimited number of missions ahead of me and each one makes it that much more likely that I will die," the crews were saying "I have only twenty-five missions to go . . . now it's only twenty-four . . . now it's only twenty-three . . . and when I get down to zero, I'll be safe!"

Of course, the fliers hadn't eliminated their fear. No sane person could fly a bombing mission over enemy territory without being afraid. But having an end in sight enabled the crews to set a boundary to their fears. They had found a way to live with their fears instead of being afraid of them. In a sense, they had coped with their fears by facing their worst nightmare—the prospect of not returning from a mission—and they had discovered how to coexist with this painful possibility.

Carrie had been listening with increasing intensity, and when I finished, she was silent for several moments. I could imagine that she was thinking about her own life and her own battles with fear, and I hoped she would see that her courage lay precisely in the fact that she had persisted in her struggles even though she was so often afraid.

We didn't talk much more that day, but a few sessions later, Carrie told me that she and Joe had started trying for a family. "I still want to do something about my panic attacks," she insisted. "But I'm not willing to put my life on hold for them." Although she was still struggling with fear, Carrie had faced her fear of fear, and now she was committed to overcoming it.

The Unreality of Fear

Evolutionary biologists have long debated the role of emotions in human life. Why do we need these pesky feelings that can bring us so much misery and anguish? Wouldn't it be better for our survival if we simply viewed the world rationally rather than letting our emotions get in the way?

One theory is that emotions provide us with the energy to act positively for our own survival. As we saw in chapter 2, fear is often a great motivator for self-protection, leading us to avoid situations, people, ideas, and dreams that might get us into trouble or cause us pain. In the days when our fears centered mainly on not

SCIENCE MATTERS

Stress Can Make You Fat!

Have you ever wondered why you tend to gain weight during stressful periods of your life, even if you've stuck rigorously to your diet and exercise plan? It's likely the work of cortisol, a stress hormone that floods your body during challenging times. Cortisol has a number of useful functions to help you cope with stress, including giving your immune system a boost. But it also causes your body to retain belly fat. In the days when starvation was a very real possibility—when "a stressful week" could include a trek across the savanna or a siege inside a cave—this was a useful response. In our own times, when stress is more likely to be psychological than physical, the fat-retaining effects of cortisol are not so welcome. You can combat the effects of cortisol with vigorous, aerobic exercise, which gives your body a chance to work off some of the stress-related energy and burn some of the excess calories you may have held on to. However, don't overexercise: that just increases the stress level and starts the cycle all over again. Work with your doctor to find a vigorous but nonstressful program that is right for you.

having enough food for the winter or avoiding attacks by wild beasts, our fears may indeed have been survival mechanisms. Undoubtedly the "fight or flight response," the stress reaction, and the feeling of anxiety might have motivated us to store our food, run from danger, and otherwise protect ourselves.

Unfortunately, our emotions are not always the best guide to reality. Sometimes our fear steers us away from trouble—but sometimes it steers us right into harm's way. As we saw in chapter 1, this may be a function of how ironic processes work: the more we want to avoid something, the more our mind ironically pushes us in that direction. "Don't slip on the ice," "Stay away from that cigarette," and "Be careful not to offend your powerful boss" can easily become irresistible compulsions to do the very thing that hurts us most. (No one has yet come up with a convincing evolutionary explanation for why those ironic processes are necessary, but I'll be fascinated to hear it if anyone ever does!)

Sometimes our fear itself is what distorts our view of reality. As we saw in chapter 2, our anxiety itself releases powerful stress hormones that can keep us from thinking rationally.

Worse, our fear tends to create a reality of its own. This is where fear of fear comes in. A study by psychologist Jennifer Wild and her colleagues suggests that people who, like Carrie, are often fearful use their fears to assess a situation rather than looking clearly at the situation itself.

Wild and her colleagues at the Department of Psychology in London's Institute of Psychiatry studied seventy-two university students who had been diagnosed as "socially anxious"—having unusually high levels of anxiety in social situations. The anxious students were asked to speak with one of three people who had been instructed to act in a pleasant but neutral manner. While engaged in conversation, the students were hooked up to a complicated apparatus and informed—falsely—that the apparatus would give them feedback about their heart rate, which they understood was a reliable indicator of their anxiety level.

In fact, the apparatus was programmed to vibrate against the students' skin once every minute or so, regardless of what actually happened during the conversation. It had no actual connection to their hearts or to any other biological measure of anxiety. And indeed, one group of students was told that the vibration indicated an increased heart rate—that is, increased anxiety on their part—while another was told that the vibration indicated a decreased heart rate—that is, a more relaxed state. A third control group was told that the vibrator wasn't measuring anything at all, that the researchers were simply checking out a new piece of equipment and wanted to know if the students had found it comfortable to wear.

After their conversations, which lasted about ten minutes, students were asked to rate both how anxious they had felt and how well they thought they'd come across to the other person. The results were illuminating. Students who had been led to believe that their anxiety was rising were far more likely to report that they were anxious—and also more likely to report that they seemed anxious. Significantly, they further tended to believe that they'd made a poor impression on the person they had spoken with.

Likewise, students who had been led to believe that they were calm and relaxed were far more likely to report that they had, indeed, felt that way. They were also more likely to report both that they'd seemed relaxed and that they had made a good impression.

In other words, participants were not reacting to how successful the conversation had actually been. Instead, they reacted to how anxious they believed they were. In their minds, being anxious meant they had performed badly; being less anxious meant they had performed well. Their assessment of reality was based not on objective evidence of reality—how the person they had spoken with actually reacted to them. It was based on how they felt. It was as if they were saying, "I can't possibly make a good impression on someone when I'm scared. Once I know I'm scared, that's the same to me as knowing that I've failed."

But as we've seen, it's perfectly possible to feel anxious and to proceed without letting that anxiety run the show. You might be able to conceal your anxiety from the person you're speaking to, and you might be able to make a good impression even if you don't. Your only way of knowing how well you came across is to pay attention to the person you're talking to and to the events that follow the conversation. In a social situation, does the person want to see you again? In a work situation, does the person give you good assignments or happily take your calls? How you feel—whether anxious or not—has absolutely no bearing on whether the other person considered the conversation successful.

How you acted, of course, may have a great deal to do with how the other person responds to you, though even then, you don't always know what actions will produce a good response. Perhaps your behaving in an anxious way makes the other person feel sympathy, or maybe he feels relieved that he's not the only one to be nervous. Perhaps your anxiety even provokes admiration: "Look how scared she is, and yet she's not giving up!" Or perhaps your anxiety, whether personal or professional, is a turn-off—but again, the only way to know that is to assess the other person's response to you. Your own anxiety levels don't tell you anything except how you feel.

If, like Carrie, you're scared of your own fear, you may have a hard time grasping this distinction. "I feel anxious," you say to yourself, "therefore the person I'm talking to perceives me as anxious." Not necessarily! Or, "I feel unworthy, therefore he perceives me as unworthy." Again, not necessarily! Your feelings are just your feelings—clues to your own experience, but not necessarily to the other person's. Hard as it is to accept, you need to realize that you really don't have any control over how others in a situation will react to you. You certainly can't judge their reactions based on your own physical responses.

Based on the observations of the three people with whom the students conversed, the students were very poor judges of the impressions they made. The students' ratings did not at all correspond with the ratings made by the observers, who were far less likely to rate the students as behaving anxiously than the students were likely to rate themselves, and far more likely to report that the students had made a good impression than the students themselves had assumed. The students made their judgments based on how they had felt during the conversation; but the observers' ratings made it quite clear that these feelings weren't an accurate foundation for making good judgments. In other words, accepting the limits of what your emotions can tell you is the first step toward freeing yourself from fear of your own fear.

E X E R C I S E

Challenge Your Fear of Fear

1. *Relax.* As always, achieve relaxation by seeing yourself moving slowly down a flight of eighteen stairs, breathing and counting at each step. Count backward, from eighteen at the top to one at the bottom.

2. *Identify a situation in which you tend to feel anxious.* You might choose a social situation, such as a party or a first date; a work experience, such as a client meeting or presentation; a family event, such as a dinner with your parents or a holiday with your siblings; or any other situation that triggers your anxiety levels.

3. *Visualize yourself in the situation.* See yourself speaking with a person or performing an activity that triggers your anxiety. Use sensory details to make your visualization feel as real to you as possible. Ask yourself what you see, hear, smell, taste, and feel, and allow yourself the time to make each sensory detail as real and as vivid as possible: the red berries on the holly wreath, for example, and the sweet, nutmeg taste of Grandma Millie's eggnog; or the smell of dry white wine and the sight of your date's fingers curled around the stem of his wineglass. You can use a specific memory of an anxious time or simply imagine an event, but either way, zero in on the details until you can feel your anxiety levels start to rise.

4. *Check in with your body.* How do you know you're anxious? See if you can notice at least five specific physical signals; for example: (1) flushed face; (2) sweaty palms; (3) pounding heart; (4) tight stomach; (5) dry throat. Don't just notice the body part; find a clear way of describing to yourself the specific change in that part of your body that indicates to you that you are anxious. Jot down at least five symptoms of anxiety.

5. *Invite your body to change.* Continue to imagine yourself in the anxiety-provoking situation, adding new details if necessary to keep your anxiety levels high. Then focus one by one on the body parts you've listed. Invite yourself to visualize each one in its relaxed or nonanxious state. Don't try to "make" it change—that will only invite your Monitor to do its ironic job, and you'll conceivably end up more anxious than before. But see if simply visualizing each body part in a relaxed state produces any change in how you feel.

6. *Shift your focus.* After a few minutes, regardless of whether your anxiety levels have decreased, increased, or remained the same, shift the focus of your visualization to another person in the scene. Allow yourself to view the scene from this other person's point of view. Ask yourself to find five specific clues in the other person's words or actions that indicate how he or she is viewing you, and jot them down. Be as specific as possible; for example: (1) smiled in a warm and friendly way; (2) rolled eyes—looked disgusted; (3) asked me for another example in a bored tone of voice; (4) asked me for a third example in a more interested tone of voice; (5) touched my elbow as he said good-bye. Keep your focus on the specifics of what you notice; not until the next step will you move on to an interpretation of what they mean.

7. *Assess the clues.* "Freeze" the scene you've been visualizing, as when you hit the pause button on your remote control. With the other person frozen in place, step out of the scene mentally and examine the list you've just made. Ask yourself how you would assess each clue separately and what you make of all of them together. Be as honest as possible, and be willing to be surprised!

8. *Ask yourself if you can act to improve the situation.* Again, be as honest as you can while remaining open to all the possibilities.

You may decide that the other person's idea of you is fixed and can't be changed. You may decide that there is something that might affect the other person, but you're unable or unwilling to do it. Or you may decide that you're perfectly happy with the situation and aren't interested in doing anything to change it. Whatever your assessment, write it down.

9. *Return to the scene.* Step back into the scene and unfreeze it. Spend a few more minutes in the conversation you've imagined. If you decided on a change of behavior, try it out and repeat steps 6 through 9 until you're satisfied that there are no other changes you want to make at this time. Remind yourself that you can always repeat the exercise another time if you like.

10. *Return to your current surroundings.* When you're ready, find a way to finish the conversation. Then imagine yourself climbing up the flight of eighteen stairs, breathing and counting at each one, from one at the bottom to eighteen at the top.

11. *Evaluate the experience.* Check in with your body—particularly the five areas you noted as the seats of your anxiety. Write down how each area is feeling now and continue to write for about five minutes, exploring what you think and how you feel about the experience you've just had.

From Our "Feeling" Mind to Our "Thinking" Mind

Part of my goal with Carrie was to help her move her fears from the part of her brain that simply experiences emotion—the limbic system—to a somewhat newer and more evolved portion of the brain that produces thought: the frontal lobes. Helping people bring their rational minds to bear on irrational emotions is a familiar part of most therapists' work, but I was happy to know that the process was supported by two experiments that I had conducted with several of my colleagues at Cornell University and the Mount Sinai School of Medicine.

In each experiment, healthy women were shown two different visual cues—squares of a different color. They were told that when they saw one color, they might receive a shock; when they saw the other color, they were safe. (In fact, no shocks were ever administered.) While they were viewing the squares, we measured their responses through a functional MRI and via a measurement of their galvanic skin response—the change in conductance of their skin. (When we feel strong emotions, we tend to sweat, making our skin better able to conduct electricity.)

What we found was that at first the women evidenced signs of anxiety and fear whenever they saw the color they associated with danger. Parts of the brain lit up—portions of the limbic system.

But as the experiments proceeded and the women felt safer, their brains responded quite differently to the "unsafe" color. The limbic area became less active, and another area, the frontal lobes, lit up instead. In other words, realizing that they could handle the anxiety inherent in the situation, the women became less emotional and more rational—just as I hoped Carrie would learn to do.

Significantly, a third experiment added a new dimension to our understanding as we included both healthy people and people who suffered from panic disorder and posttraumatic stress disorder (PTSD). We found that the healthy people's brains were most active when they were being shown the unsafe color—when they believed they had to gear up to protect themselves during a time when they might be hurt. But the more fearful people who suffered from panic disorder and PTSD showed relatively less brain activity in response to the unsafe color and more in response to the safe color.

In other words, the healthy people assumed the world was a pretty safe place. Their brains went on high alert only when they had good reason to suspect they might be facing danger. But the fearful people were used to viewing the world as a threatening environment. Their brains grew more active not in response to danger, which they expected, but in response to safety, which they did not. They were actually more upset—or, at least, more mentally active and on guard—in response to safety than to a genuine potential for being hurt.

As both therapist and neuroscientist, I consider these results extremely significant. Although it's too soon to draw any firm conclusions, I have the feeling that for most of us, there are certain fears and anxieties—either fear of our own fear, or perhaps one of the other fears considered in part two—that affect us especially deeply. When these fears are in play—when our fear of envy or isolation or of not being a real man or a real woman is triggered—we become, in a way, like a person suffering from panic disorder or PTSD, even if we haven't been diagnosed with those conditions. Still, like them, we flip our view of the world from a pretty safe place where danger is unusual, to a generally threatening place where safety is unusual. We feel threatened, panicked, and paralyzed by our fears. And, like the panic-disordered and PTSD people in my study, we find ourselves unable to move our experience of fear from the emotional to the rational area of the brain. In technical terms, we are unable to form a healthy habituation to the possibility of being hurt. Paralyzed by past traumas—the man who betrayed us, the job that didn't work out, the humiliating family scene—we become literally irrational, unable to invoke the thinking, analyzing part of our brains. Instead, we become mired in emotion—and then, like the people in Jennifer Wild's study, we assume that our emotions about ourselves ("I feel anxious," "I feel panicked") are giving us accurate information about reality ("There is good reason for me to feel so scared—I am facing a major threat").

But our fear is playing us false. It's not really giving us accurate information about the world; it's not even giving us accurate information about ourselves. To see more about how fear can distort our self-concept, let's look at another study of Israeli soldiers.

Israeli soldiers are routinely trained early on to carry a heavy pack while marching very quickly over a distance of approximately thirty miles. In the study I am about to describe, the soldiers were divided into four groups:

- *Group 1 was given true and full information.* They were told that they would be marching only about thirty miles (true information) and were continually told how far they had left to go (full information). In that sense, they were treated like the U.S. flight crews after the policy change, who were told that they had only twenty-five missions to fly, which the crews then began to count.

- *Group 2 was given no information.* They were simply told to put on their packs and start marching. Eventually, presumably, they would be told to stop, but for all they knew, they'd be commanded to keep marching indefinitely. In that sense, they were a bit like the U.S. flight crews before the policy change.

- *Group 3 was given first encouraging, then discouraging information.* They were told they would march only about eighteen miles. But then, just as they were almost done with their trek, they were told they would have to march an additional twelve miles, for a total of thirty miles, the distance they had been trained to do.

- *Group 4 was given first discouraging, then encouraging information.* They were told they would march for about forty-three miles. Then, just as they, too, had reached almost eighteen miles, they were told that instead, they would march for only thirty miles—again, the distance they had been trained to do.

How did the soldiers' fears affect their beliefs about what they were capable of?

Group 1 participants, who knew exactly what they were up against, were far more likely to complete the task than Group 2 participants, who had no idea what they were facing. Theoretically, the two randomly selected groups should have been equally capable of completing any task, particularly one they had already trained for. But apparently the soldiers without information found themselves disabled by the anxiety of not knowing what was to come and therefore being unable to decide if they were capable of it.

Group 4 participants—who expected to be faced with the most difficult task—performed the worst. Again, remember, everyone had had the same training, so in theory, everyone should have performed equally well. Yet the Group 4 participants, expecting to be faced with a longer trek than they thought they could handle, found themselves exhausted and incapacitated early in the march. In fact, 10 percent dropped out after only about six miles—even though they'd often marched five times that far in previous training sessions. They couldn't bear thinking about how far they had to go—in fact, thinking about it turned out to be harder to bear than the actual weight of their backpacks! And since they ultimately didn't have to go as far as they first believed, all that disabling anxiety was over a situation that didn't even come to pass. How many times have we all experienced that?!

Likewise, Group 3, believing that they were in for a task they knew they could handle, started out very high in morale. But when they were given the discouraging information about how much more they'd have to do than they thought—even though it was a distance they knew they could do—their morale dropped precipitously. Within fifty or sixty seconds of being given the information, they began to show evidence of depression: slouching, ceasing to talk to each other, and so on. Soon, many of the participants in this group began dropping out—well before they'd covered the thirty miles they had been trained to march.

By the same token, the remaining soldiers in Group 4—those few who hadn't yet dropped out—brightened considerably upon hearing that they wouldn't have to go as far as they'd thought. In fact, everyone in the group who was still marching at that point made it to the finish line.

Clearly, our expectations of failure and success have an enormous amount to do with whether we succeed—far more, apparently, than our actual ability to get the job done. Remember, all the soldiers in the study had demonstrated countless times that they could march thirty miles—when they knew that was all they'd have to do. But altering their expectations and creating a situation in which they felt helpless, out of control, and at their commanders' mercy literally disabled them, keeping them from completing a task they were fully capable of.

In my view, this experiment makes clear that fear of fear is one of our most disabling emotions. The experiment also demonstrates that our emotions—fear, frustration, despair—are often highly inaccurate guides to our actual situation. As it happened, no one in the study actually had to do more than he had already shown he could do. But many people in the study believed they would have to do more—and so, most of the time, they did even less.

If this is the response of a team of highly motivated men who have a great deal of peer and family pressure to do well in this situation, imagine how much more likely the rest of us are to succumb to the fear of our own fear. In my view, we can draw three key lessons from this study, as well as from my own research into anxiety:

1. Quite often, what we fear—the shocks, the forty-three-mile hike—never comes to pass, no matter what we've been told or led to believe. Yet our emotions can lead us to be gullible, gearing up in response to whatever information we've been given.

2. These emotions tend to create their own reality. Believing that something bad is going to happen, they often ensure that it

will—indeed, they often ensure that something even worse will happen. (Soldiers who could theoretically march thirty miles were suddenly unable to manage even six.)

3. Since we often don't have accurate or complete information at the start of the process (whether we'll be shocked, how far we have to march), we shouldn't try to argue with our fears ("The shock won't be so bad," "I'm sure you can march forty-three miles if you try!"). Instead, we should disengage from our anxiety, allowing it to exist but not responding to it. There's often no point in trying to make ourselves feel less anxious; ironic processes will often ensure that trying to reduce anxiety only increases it. If you are interested in reducing anxiety, trying to put your fears into perspective is probably the best way to go—and often that will work. But if it doesn't, we're better off simply acknowledging our anxiety and then refusing to engage it, like a pesky dog who keeps begging us for a treat from the table. Say no once, maybe twice, perhaps even three times. Then after that, let the dog beg all he wants. You may not be able to send him away—but you don't have to feed him, either.

SCIENCE MATTERS

Stress and Stereotypes

Another study of pilots has produced some rather disturbing information for those who often fly. In a study demonstrating how people might not be rational when under stress, Shlomo Breznitz describes reports of how professional pilots responded to unexpected and potentially catastrophic events. Surprisingly, all the pilots had the same story: when confronted with a catastrophic problem, they tried to correct the situation by pressing the buttons they'd assume were responsible for the system failure. And when that didn't work, they tended to press them again and again, each time more forcefully. Researchers concluded that at moments of greatest stress, we are least able to come up with new ideas, even though that's usually when we need them the most! That's why pilots and other people charged with lots of responsibility are encouraged to make emergency responses routine—to repeat them even in nonemergency situations so that when the real thing occurs, a stereotypic response will be second nature.

For those who don't shoulder such big responsibilities, we can take away another lesson: don't expect yourself (or anyone else) to come up with a good response to a stressful situation when you're right in the middle of it, because that's when you're least likely to discover new ways to cope. Work on your coping skills before the crisis strikes—and during the crisis, get plenty of help from friends; family; loved ones; and, if necessary, a therapist, because that's when you're least able to devise new strategies for yourself.

EXERCISE
Disengage from Your Anxiety

1. *Relax.* Use deep breathing to relax your body and clear your mind. As always, visualize descending a flight of stairs as you breathe and count down.

2. *Visualize a situation that makes you anxious.* As in the previous exercise, use specific sensory details—from sight, hearing, smell, taste, and sensation—to bring the situation into focus and allow your emotions to arise.

3. *Visualize your anxiety itself.* See your anxiety literally floating out of your body and coming to rest alongside it. Take some time to give form to your anxiety. What color is it? What shape?

Is it transparent? Solid? Does it have a smell? Is it getting bigger? Smaller? Shinier? Darker? Lighter? Is it changing in some other way? Does it look like a person, animal, or object you recognize? Take some time to respond to your anxiety with each of your five senses.

4. *Create a shield to keep your anxiety at a safe distance.* Accept your anxiety's presence in this instance, but choose the distance at which you would like it to remain. Be very specific, as you envision the scene, about where you would like your anxiety to be while you are continuing your business. Having chosen that distance, visualize some kind of device that will maintain it for you—a shield, a force field, a fluffy white cloud, a burst of blue light—whatever you can visualize to maintain the distance you have chosen.

5. *Continue your activity in the scene.* Whatever you were doing when your anxiety left your body, continue. While you continue, notice your anxiety's behavior and your own response. Commit to maintaining the distance you have chosen, and, if necessary, experiment with different ways to do so.

6. *Conclude the scene.* When you are ready, find a way to end the scene you are imagining. Return to your actual surroundings by ascending the imaginary stairs, breathing and counting.

7. *Check in with your body.* Notice how you are feeling now. Be aware that the more you practice specific, physical check-ins with your body, the easier you are likely to master your anxiety. Anxiety thrives on vague feelings, a sense of disconnectedness, and a confused mind. A sharp, precise observation of your physical self is a terrific way to set boundaries on your feelings of worry and fear.

8. *Write about the experience.* As always, taking at least five minutes to process what you've learned is an excellent way to consolidate your new memories and reshape your old ones. (For

more on the consolidation and reconsolidation of memories, see pages 69–70 and 166.)

Mastering Other Fears

In this chapter, we've explored a fear that tends to compound all the others: fear of fear itself. Throughout the rest of part two, we'll explore five other hidden fears that can lead you to sabotage yourself, keeping you from getting the life you really want.

CHAPTER 5

Free Yourself from Your Fear of Guilt

The fear of guilt can be one of the most powerful of all our hidden fears. I know, because one of my own most challenging experiences involved this painful and often confusing emotion.

It happened while I was just about to finish graduate school. By now, I had confirmed that graduate school in psychology was indeed a perfect match for me. I loved learning about the human mind, conducting research into the ways that our brains produce awareness, insight, and emotion. I loved studying psychotherapy and finding out how I could help people create the lives they really wanted. And I genuinely enjoyed the professors and students with whom I studied.

All except one. There was one professor with whom I seemed to always bump heads—and unfortunately for me, she was my adviser, my committee chair. I had always gotten on well with a wide variety of people, but for some reason, this woman and I always had a very difficult time seeing eye-to-eye. Sure, she was brilliant and I learned a lot from her—but the process certainly wasn't easy for me. Still, I proceeded with my work, and I was proud of the thesis I was about to submit.

Suddenly, just before I was about to complete that final, crucial requirement to get my degree, I began to experience a tremendous amount of anxiety. It seemed to come completely out of the blue. I'd wake up in the middle of the night, my heart racing, my mind preoccupied with an upsetting dream I could no longer remember. Or I'd be sitting at my desk, trying to put the final touches on my thesis, and my mind would just freeze up, preoccupied with a thousand fears and worries that I could never quite grasp. At the movies, at a party, even in the shower, there was no escape from the overwhelming anxiety. I couldn't understand where these feelings were coming from, but they were becoming nearly unbearable.

Then, out of the blue, I found myself involved in an intense, out-of-control argument with my committee chair. I stood in her office and literally screamed at her, telling her how little help she was being, how she was constantly putting up roadblocks that were making it increasingly harder for me to graduate, how angry I was with her. In my entire life, I had never had a meltdown like that (and fortunately, I've never had one since!). It seemed to come from nowhere.

I was just on the verge of telling her that I planned to quit the program—to walk away from the past five years of hard work and committed learning—when fortunately, somehow, I stopped myself. Instead, I just turned around and walked out.

Like virtually everyone who plans to become a therapist, I had a therapist of my own. (How else can you adequately offer help to your patients who are wrestling with issues like yours?) So the next day I went to my regular session with him and tried to figure out what had happened. I'm sure my therapist understood everything right away, but as all good therapists do, he let me struggle with my own conflicted feelings as I tried to figure it out for myself.

The only conclusion I came to in that session was that I really didn't want to abandon my studies and the profession I had come to love. I had worked far too hard to throw away my entire career for a stupid argument I didn't even understand. I had to go back and patch things up with my adviser.

Luckily for me, my adviser was forgiving and compassionate, and seemed more than willing to help me with the last few steps involved in getting my degree. And eventually I came to see that my fear of guilt was the hidden fear behind both my anxiety and my unexpected outburst—the guilt I bore toward my father. My father had always wanted to get an advanced degree and had dreamed of becoming a professor, and I think he would have loved to create a life like mine. He had gone to graduate school and was working on his master's degree when his own father said, "You have to come into the family business." Obediently, he gave up his own dreams to follow those of his father. All he could do was promise himself that when he became a father, he would never do the same thing to his son.

And he never did. My father always supported me in every way possible, and I've always been grateful for that support. But I guess I've always felt guilty about it, too. How could I take what was out of his reach? How could I go places he wasn't allowed to go? What if he was angry with me? What if he resented me? What if my achievements made him feel as though his life was less valuable?

In fact, I think he did feel a little bit like that. Last year, as he was in the throes of his final illness, we spoke about these issues for the first time. While my father was clearly not angry with me, I could see that he felt a certain sorrow over what he hadn't been able to accomplish, along with his pride in having been able to help me. I don't think my guilt was warranted, because I don't think I did anything wrong—and my father certainly didn't think

I had. But the whole experience has helped me see how deeply these feelings run and how mysteriously they can express themselves. I had no idea when I was shouting at my adviser that what was really going on was hidden guilt over my father—a guilt that might have led me to give up my own chance to achieve the goals he had never been able to reach. How much better I could have handled that situation if only I'd been able to identify my hidden fears. (And how disastrous it would have been had I not had a therapist!)

The Power of Guilt

Fear of guilt may be one of the most powerful of our hidden fears, because by definition it's often the one we're least willing to look at. If we think we've done something wrong and we don't want to face it, we not only feel guilty, but we also bury our guilt. That buried guilt can produce all sorts of mysterious behavior that should let us know there's a three-hundred-pound gorilla in the room. Instead, most of us—myself included!—often try even harder to bury the guilt and ignore our own self-sabotaging responses to it.

From a therapist's perspective, guilt is especially tricky because it's not actually an emotion; it's what happens when we ignore an emotion. The primary feeling is anger; the guilt is anger turned inward.

How does this work? In my case, I was saddened that my father didn't have a more satisfying career and that it wasn't in my power to give him as much as he'd given me. I felt helpless because I couldn't help him. Then I felt angry because I didn't like feeling helpless. It was as though I were saying, "Why couldn't you have had a more satisfying career so I wouldn't have to feel bad for you?" Then I turned that anger inward, where it became guilt: "How can I throw my accomplishments and the joys of my new profession into the face of a man who spent his whole working life in a job that he hated, just so he could take care of his family and say that he did the honorable thing?"

In a funny way, guilt was my way of taking power in a situation where I was really powerless. Although I couldn't make my father any happier—I couldn't go back in time and pay for his graduate school or force his father to support my father's dream—I could turn the anger I felt about that against myself, in effect pretending that I could make him happier. My guilt was a way of saying, "I'm so powerful, I could make my father happier—and since I'm not doing it, I must be a bad person." To me, thinking of myself as a bad person was easier than admitting the truth: my beloved father had some major regrets about his life, and there was nothing I could do to ease his pain.

Miriam, whom we've met in earlier chapters, had a similar problem of guilt with regard to her mother. In Miriam's case, her mother compounded the problem by actually blaming Miriam for her mother's unhappiness. Both mother and daughter agreed: if Miriam's mother was unhappy, Miriam must be at fault. These dynamics all went on under the surface, so that neither woman was consciously aware of them. Nevertheless, Miriam was going along with her mother's view of her as a very powerful person who was responsible for her mother's happiness.

For Miriam, as for so many of us, the guilt that followed was preferable to admitting the truth: she really had very little to do with whether her mother was happy or not, especially with regard to her mother's being single. Miriam couldn't find a good husband for her mother. She couldn't go back in time and make her own father into a better man. She couldn't erase her mother's feelings of failure, loneliness, and despair. And she couldn't really make her mother any happier by not finding a man of her own. Only Miriam's mother could change her life situation and her feelings about her life. Miriam had no control over that situation, whether she found herself a good man or not.

To me, it was clear that Miriam had no control over her mother's situation and therefore no reason to feel guilt. But for Miriam, fear of her own lack of control was yet another feeling she didn't want to face. Rather than accept her powerlessness to change her mother's life, she preferred to see herself as powerful enough to "save" her mother—and then to feel guilty about not doing it. The price she paid was to have every one of her relationships mysteriously fail.

Miriam didn't realize why she kept herself out of good relationships any more than I had realized why I had felt so anxious or why I'd risked my career by fighting over nothing with my adviser. But that's because both of us were refusing to look at our hidden fears.

Is fear of guilt one of your hidden fears? If so, you may find the following exercise extremely helpful.

EXERCISE
Challenge Your Fear of Guilt

1. *Choose a person about whom you feel guilty.* If you're not sure whom to choose, look over the following questions. Notice who pops automatically into mind as you read them. Choose either the first person you think of or the person about whom you feel most strongly:

    - Is there someone you could have helped recently whom you did not?

    - Is there someone you feel does more for you than you return?

    - Is there someone in your life who is unhappy and whom you wish you could make happier?

    - Is there someone in your life who you feel needs you in ways you don't always come through for?

- Is there someone with whom you are often fighting or quarreling? (That's often—though not always—a sign of guilt!)

Remember, I'm not saying you should feel guilty about anyone who comes to mind—or about anyone at all! I'm only trying to help you identify someone about whom you may feel guilty.

2. *Identify your own guilty feelings.* Again, your feelings don't necessarily reflect reality. You may feel as though something were true when it isn't actually true. But for the moment, focus only on what you feel, not on what you think. Bring your own feelings into focus by completing the following sentences, quickly, off the top of your head:

- When I think of [person], I feel guilty because _____ _____.
- I wish I could do more for [person] because _____ _____.
- [Person] needs me because _____ _____.
- I have made life harder for [person] because _____ _____.
- If I were a better person, something I would do for [person] is _____.
- If I were a better person, when I think of [person], I would feel only _____.
- If I were a better person, when I deal with [person], I would never _____.
- In the ideal world, my relationship with [person] would be _____.
- In the ideal world, [person] would have _____ _____.

3. *Look objectively at the person you feel guilty about.* Forget for the moment about your own feelings. Focus instead on the person you feel guilty about, and think of what's missing in his or her life. Don't ask yourself what you could do to make that person happy; don't even ask yourself what he or she believes would bring happiness. Just ask yourself what, in your opinion, would genuinely make that person happy: More friends? A husband or a wife? A better job? A closer community? A different attitude? Take as much time as you need to write down your answer, and be as specific as possible. If you decide that getting married will make this person happy, for example, specify what kind of partner it would have to be. If you think he or she needs more money, put a dollar amount on it or describe it in another way: "enough to take a two-week vacation every year," "enough to pay off all debts," "enough to retire on at his or her current standard of living."

Remember, you're only listing elements that actually will make this person happy. If she says she'd love you to visit more, but isn't actually happier when you do, don't put down "visit more"! If he is always complaining about financial security but in your opinion will never feel secure no matter how much money he has, don't put down "more money." Only put down what you think will actually make this person happier.

4. *Look objectively at your own power.* Reread what you've written about what you think would really make this person happy. With a red pen or brightly colored marker, highlight each part of what you wrote that is realistically in your power to accomplish. If you could not fulfill that wish but believe you could help with it—for example, you can't find a husband for a lonely woman, but you could take her shopping for a more attractive wardrobe or show her how to sign up for a dating service—put a star by the item and write a footnote explaining precisely what is in your power to do.

5. *Look objectively at your own wishes.* Look at the items you have marked. If you are already doing some, copy them onto a separate page labeled "What I'm Already Doing." If there are some that you theoretically could do but feel are clearly out of the question—for example, driving two hours to the person's house two evenings a week to help her get ready for dates—copy them onto a page labeled "What I'm Not Willing to Do." Copy the remaining items onto a third page, labeled "What I Might Be Willing to Do."

6. *Decide what additional difference you might make.* Look at the list labeled "What I Might Be Willing to Do." Go down the list, item by item. For each one, ask yourself, "How much difference would this make in the problem?" For example, maybe you've decided that something you might do is to take your person shopping for a new, more attractive wardrobe. But is the lack of a wardrobe really the reason why she's not in a good relationship? Does she need you to help her choose new clothes? Could she do it alone, or with other people? Would she allow you to help her, or would the trip end in frustration for both of you, with no real improvement in her wardrobe—or in her romantic prospects? After considering each item in this way, put a rating beside it, using the following scale:

   1 = would basically make little or no difference
   2 = might make some difference, but a lot of other things would need to change
   3 = might make some difference
   4 = might turn the whole situation around
   5 = would definitely solve the problem

7. *Evaluate your ratings.* Look at the items you've marked and how you've scored them. Realistically, what can you do that you're not already doing to make things better for the

person you feel guilty about? Is there anything that might make a genuine difference that you're still not willing to do? Make a new list—"What I Now Commit to Doing"—and put down any new actions that you now decide you're willing to take. Remember, you're listing only actions that you genuinely believe will make a difference. Add any other items that might make a difference but that you won't do onto your list "What I'm Not Willing to Do."

8. *Explore your willingness.* Look at the list of what you're not willing to do. Write for at least five minutes about why you are not willing to do the things you've identified. Be honest about your own feelings, needs, and limits.

9. *Accept your limits.* When you've completed this process, you may discover that there is nothing you can do to make things better for the person you've chosen. Or you may discover that there are some things you can do and, as a result, commit to doing them. Or perhaps you'll find that there are some things you could do that, for whatever reason, you're not willing to do. Whatever you decide, help put your feelings into perspective by completing the following sentences. In this case, I urge you to answer each question thoughtfully, taking full responsibility for everything you write:

   - Something I wish I could do for [person] that I accept I can't is _____.
   - Something that would be good to do for [person] that I accept I won't is _____.
   - Something I wish I could change about [person] that I accept I can't is _____.
   - When I realize that I don't have the power to make [person] completely happy, I feel _____
   _____.
   - Something that would help me accept my limits is _____
   _____.

10. *Accept your feelings.* How does accepting your limits make you feel? If you're like most of us, you're likely to feel some combination of sorrow, anger, frustration, and relief. These feelings may change over time, particularly if doing this exercise is the first time you've confronted them. I recommend writing about how you feel for at least five minutes a day for the next two weeks.

Other Ways to Overcome Guilt

- *Meditate.* Meditation can have extraordinary benefits in helping us to accept our limits, our feelings, and the things we don't have the power to change. You can take a class at a local yoga center, Buddhist temple, or adult-education center.

- *Meditate through motion.* Yoga and tai chi are excellent forms of "moving meditation" that accomplish many of the same benefits as seated meditation. You can also find examples of moving meditation in *Light on Life: The Yoga Journey to Wholeness, Inner Peace, and Ultimate Freedom* and *Light on Yoga*, both by B. K. S. Iyengar.

- *Work with a support group.* Many support groups, including twelve-step programs, are designed to help people cope with guilt. Check in your Yellow Pages, do an online search, or ask at a local mental health center or community center to see if there's a support group that fits your needs.

- *Work with a counselor or a therapist.* A therapist can often help you make faster and more solid progress than you're able to make alone. If you feel that guilt has become a disabling force in your life, consider finding someone to help you put it in perspective.

SCIENCE MATTERS

Meditation Literally Alters Your Brain

I'll admit it: in my own personal experience, meditation has not been a particularly effective tool for me. But I'm vastly impressed by what it seems to do for other people. I was particularly struck by a study I read by a standout team of researchers from such topflight institutions as Massachusetts General Hospital, Harvard and Yale universities, and Beth Israel Deaconness Hospital in Boston, led by Sarah W. Lazar. The researchers used MRI scans to measure the brains of twenty individuals who had had extensive experience with meditation. They found a distinct thickening in parts of the prefrontal cortex (the region of the brain associated with rational thought), specifically, some of the areas involved in attention, interoception (a scientific term meaning "responsiveness to external stimuli), and sensory processing. The thickening was especially notable among older meditators, since the prefrontal cortex tends to thin with age, suggesting that perhaps meditation has this significant antiaging benefit. Moreover, the degree of thickness corresponded to the length of time people had been meditating.

For those who study this part of the brain, these data are extremely exciting. First, they provided the first structural evidence that meditation does indeed seem to affect the physical nature of our brains. Second, they focused on the insula, an area of the brain that links outside experience with internal processing (an area I have studied), suggesting that meditation results in a better understanding of the relationship between our inner world and the outer world. Finally, since meditation presumably helped to develop the prefrontal cortex, we can speculate that meditation might enhance many other cognitive functions, including memory and "approach/withdrawal behavior" (our decisions about when to approach and when to withdraw from a person or a situation).

Envy, Hostility, and Guilt

So far, we've focused on guilt from the perspective of the person who feels guilty. But what about the person who instills guilt? As we've seen with Miriam's mother, some people actively invite their loved ones, friends, or colleagues to feel guilty, openly or covertly blaming these other people for their own pain. When these "guilt-provokers" are your own parents, it can be especially difficult to disentangle the mixed messages you may be getting. Figuring out what's really going on becomes harder still if what upsets your parents is your success.

Miriam, for example, was not consciously aware of how upset her mother had become every time Miriam talked about a man who might offer her a good, stable relationship. But on some unconscious level, Miriam had registered her mother's distress. Miriam's mother probably also didn't realize the signals she was sending out. Still, every time Miriam had good relationship news to report, she noticed without realizing it that a flicker of anger, panic, or resentment flashed across her mother's face before being replaced with her mother's usual loving smile.

My patient Dave had a similar experience with his father. A top baseball player, Dave had been in training for as long as he could remember—and for much of his childhood, his father had been his coach. As far as Dave understood consciously, his father was his biggest supporter. Certainly Dave's father had spent hundreds of hours helping his son to achieve athletic excellence. Yet Dave felt tremendously guilty about his success, believing on some level that his own achievements wounded his father, who in his youth had tried and failed to reach similar goals. Although Dave's father usually presented a smiling, positive face whenever Dave played well, Dave picked up flickers of anger and resentment, causing him to feel guilty without knowing why. As a result, Dave had begun choking every time he came to bat,

turning a potentially outstanding batting average into a suddenly poor performance.

How is it possible for us to pick up these parental cues without
being aware of them? A study by the Swedish researchers Arne
Ohman and Joaquim J. F. Soares holds the key. Ohman and Soares
explored the process of what they called "preattentive perceptual
analysis"—the ability of our brains to perceive and analyze something before we have consciously attended to it. They concluded
that our bodies respond to images that frighten us, even when we
aren't aware that this process is happening, let alone what is provoking it.

The researchers conducted their study with a group of college
students, some of whom were phobic (unusually fearful) about
snakes or spiders, and some of whom were not. The subjects were
hooked up to machines that measured their skin conductance—
as we saw, the electrical activity on their skin, long accepted as
an indicator of a powerful emotional response. Then they were
shown—very briefly (for 33 milliseconds)—a number of images,
including those of spiders and snakes, all of which were immediately followed by a second, neutral image. Without the second
image, the first one, even in its brief appearance, would have been
easy to see and consciously identify. But because the second image
appeared so quickly after the first, it masked the first one, render-
ing it imperceivable.

The masking meant that participants in the experiments had
no conscious idea which image came before the mask. Nevertheless, a significant number of the fearful subjects had a physical response—increased skin conductance—to either the masked spider
or the masked snake, whichever one triggered their phobias, while
the nonfearful subjects had no such response. In other words, even
though the phobic subjects had no conscious memory of seeing
either a spider or a snake, their brains somehow knew that they
had, and their bodies responded accordingly.

Moreover, the phobic subjects recognized that they had become anxious and distressed in response to their viewing even if they didn't understand why. When given self-assessment tests afterward about how they felt, phobic subjects rated themselves as more aroused, more disliking of what they had seen, and less in control when they had been exposed to the creatures they feared—either spiders or snakes. Nonphobic subjects didn't have such fluctuating responses; they pretty much viewed all the images with the same emotion. In fact, the phobic subjects reacted with greater emotion to the masked images than they had in an earlier experiment with unmasked images, suggesting that we are especially upset by what we pick up unconsciously but can't be sure we've seen.

To explain their findings, the researchers cited a classic principle in psychology, that our bodies respond before we're conscious of what has happened. If we never do bring the reason for our fear into consciousness—if the snake or spider or other fearful image is never consciously perceived—we may feel "overwhelmed by an automatic, inevitable fear," as the researchers put it. "Consequently," they continue, "attempts to voluntarily control [our fear] appear fruitless, and the only action alternative is to flee the situation."

In other words, if Miriam wasn't consciously aware of her mother's angry responses to Miriam's romantic success, her only action alternative was to flee the situation—by sabotaging all her potentially good relationships. If Dave wasn't consciously aware of his father's resentment of Dave's athletic success, his only action alternative was to flee the situation—by choking every time he came to bat.

Do you think that you, too, may have picked up subtle parental cues that have imperceptibly taught you to fear your own success in love, work, friendship, personal life, or some other area? If so, the following exercise may help bring some of those experiences into your awareness.

EXERCISE
Visualize a Success from Your Past

1. *Relax.* Visualize descending a flight of eighteen stairs to calm and clear your mind. As always, breathe at each step and count down from eighteen to one.

2. *Visualize a childhood or teenage situation in which you achieved some success that your parents knew about.* Allow your mind to wander over your past until you settle on a childhood or teenage scene in which you succeeded or even simply talked about succeeding in an area where you now feel frustration. You want to choose a scene in which one or both parents were aware of your actual or imagined success. When you have settled on the scene, use specific sensory details—from sight, hearing, smell, taste, and sensation—to bring the situation into focus and allow your memory to sharpen.

3. *Visualize one parent's response.* When you have the scene firmly in mind, move your attention to focus on one parent's response. Keep your sensory antennae up, noticing details that you see, hear, smell, taste, and touch, but focus primarily on your parent's face and body.

4. *Check in with your own body.* As you watch them from this distance, notice your own physical response. Has your breathing quickened? Is your chest tight? How does your stomach feel? Your throat? Your hands? Notice your physical response to this memory even if you can't give a reason for the response.

5. *If both parents are involved, shift your attention to the other parent.* Repeat steps 3 and 4 by focusing first on the other parent, then on your own bodily experience.

6. *Identify your emotional response.* Ask yourself how you are feeling now. Do you feel angry? Sad? Anxious? Relieved? Are you

noticing that you feel happy? Powerful? Exhilarated? Or do you feel weak? Regretful? Guilty?

7. *Conclude the scene.* When you are ready, find a way to end the scene you are imagining and return to your actual surroundings by slowly climbing the flight of stairs as you breathe and count.

8. *Check in with your body and your emotions.* Once again, notice how you are feeling now. If you find yourself thinking about something seemingly unrelated or irrelevant, pay special attention—those "meaningless" thoughts and images are often the best keys to what's really going on inside.

9. *Write about the experience.* Take at least five minutes to record how you feel now. Be sure to note any thoughts, feelings, or images that float by—especially the "silly" ones! Don't judge or analyze; just record.

10. *Process what you've learned.* After you've recorded your responses, you can take another five minutes to write about what you think. What has this experience taught you about your responses to your parents' responses? What have you learned about the roots of your own feelings of guilt? As with the previous exercise, I recommend writing about this subject for at least five minutes a day for the next two weeks. You can also repeat the exercise with different incidents.

What Do We Owe to Others?

My patient Emily struggled with another type of guilt: the sense that by seeking a happy life for herself, she was somehow betraying her family. As with Miriam, Dave, and me, Emily's guilt did not emerge consciously, but rather made itself felt as a powerful but unacknowledged force.

Emily was a top-of-the-line real estate agent who had worked extremely hard to build her wealthy client base and her outstanding reputation in the industry. Recently, though, she'd been plagued by an odd series of mishaps: oversleeping before an important closing, coming down with a serious cold just as a major client was coming to town, having to leave work early with a migraine. In distress, she came to me.

It soon emerged that Emily felt guilty about living in New York while the rest of her closely knit Irish family all lived near one another in a small town outside Philadelphia. Emily had managed the separation for the past ten years or so—and then her widowed mother had a stroke. While all the rest of the brothers and sisters pitched in to help take care of her, Emily just sent money. Although Emily didn't want to return to small-town life or to a daily involvement with her family, she felt guilty about remaining where she was. Instead of facing her guilt head-on, Emily buried it—and the self-sabotaging series of minor illnesses and absences was the result.

As we talked further, Emily revealed that she had a brother, Mark, who also lived far from the family. A serviceman, Mark and his family lived wherever the navy stationed him. I asked Emily whether under the circumstances, Mark had considered asking for a posting closer to the family or even leaving the service.

"Not as far as I know," Emily said. When I asked her why Mark was free to pursue his dreams while she felt guilty about pursuing hers, she looked at me in shock. "But he's not pursuing his dreams," she corrected me. "He's sacrificing himself for a greater good."

"So the issue isn't being there for your mother," I said. "It's who's sacrificing herself and who's not."

Emily shook her head. "I never quite thought of it like that," she said. "But I guess maybe you're right. If I was doing something for other people, something big, like Mark, maybe I could stay in New York. But if all I'm doing is enjoying myself, then how can I be so selfish?"

Don't get me wrong. I'm all for people making sacrifices—for their loved ones, for a cause, in pursuit of a larger dream. And had Emily consciously decided to return to her family, perhaps she would have been making the decision that was right for her. Under the circumstances, though, I felt that Emily's actions spoke of how much she wished to remain in New York—even as her fear of guilt led her to sabotage herself. Even if Emily were to decide that she needed to return to Pennsylvania, I thought she would be happier with her decision if she made it consciously, rather than slinking back home in defeat after destroying the career she'd worked so hard to build. I also wanted her to understand that working for ourselves and our own satisfaction isn't necessarily wrong—that we have a right to that kind of fulfillment, even if sometimes we also have to make sacrifices.

Is a fear of guilt over not sacrificing enough one of your hidden fears? Take the following quiz to find out more.

QUIZ
What's Your Relationship to Self-Sacrifice?

1. You have a precious free evening—your first in two weeks. You're looking forward to a few hours of alone time when your sister calls. "Remember how you promised to babysit?" she says. "Well, Joe and I just got invited to a party—and we haven't been out of the house in months! Can you come over tonight? The kids would love to see you!" You say:
   a. "No problem, I'll be right there! Can I bring anything?"
   b. "How about if I pay for a babysitter instead? And if you can't find one, then I'll come over."
   c. "I'm so sorry, but tonight really isn't good for me. Can we make a date now for another time?"

    d. "I will babysit for you, but only if you give me a little more notice."

2. You have an important date this weekend, and your one chance to buy a new outfit is tonight, while your favorite store is still open. You've worked at triple speed all day to make sure your work is done by 5:00 P.M. Just as you're about to dash out the door, a coworker stops you. "I'm really up against it," she says. "My secretary's out, the photocopy machine keeps jamming, and my computer keeps crashing. Please, can you stay and help me get my presentation ready for tomorrow morning? I'm desperate!" You say:

    a. "Sure, how can I help?"

    b. "I'll stay for exactly thirty minutes—then I have to dash or I'll be late myself."

    c. "I'm really sorry—I just can't tonight. If it would help, I'll come in early tomorrow, though."

    d. "So sorry—I just can't tonight."

3. You find yourself with an unexpected free hour. You use it to

    a. do an errand for your kids;

    b. return a phone call that has been weighing on your mind;

    c. indulge yourself in a rare treat—a soak in the tub, a quiet cup of coffee, some pleasure reading;

    d. leave your family a note saying you won't be home for dinner and turn that one hour into four.

4. Volunteers at your children's school are dividing up tasks for the yearly fund-raiser. At the meeting are several parents who you know are even busier and more stressed than you are, including the three mothers of disabled children; a recently widowed, newly single father; and two low-income parents who almost never make it to these meetings. Also present are three mothers with no jobs and full-time housekeepers, and a father

who hasn't contributed to a single school event the whole time you've known him. You volunteer for

    a. any assignment that no one else will take;

    b. two difficult assignments and one easy one;

    c. one difficult assignment;

    d. one easy assignment.

5. You have the chance to take a ten-week class on a topic that has always interested you. For you to attend, though, your husband would have to come home early on a night that he has scheduled for a weekly racquetball game. You

    a. immediately forgo the class;

    b. ask the teacher if you could come every other week;

    c. ask your husband if he could reschedule his game and/ or work with you to find a sitter;

    d. inform your husband that you've signed up for the class.

Answers

If most of your answers were (a), you seem to have a very difficult time putting yourself before others. Sometimes sacrifice is important—but you're important, too! Has fear of guilt begun to control your life?

If most of your answers were (b), you seem to be ambivalent: on the one hand, you'd like to nurture yourself; on the other hand, your guilt keeps you from going all the way. Consider whether you might tip the balance a bit further in favor of self-nurture.

If most of your answers were (c), then congratulations! You seem to have a healthy relationship to self-nurturing. If you also find yourself feeling guilty, check out the exercise "Challenge Your Fear of Guilt" beginning on page 110.

If most of your answers were (d), you've clearly mastered the art of setting boundaries and caring for yourself—bravo! Now consider whether you might benefit from being more open to negotiation, particularly if you are feeling guilty or ambivalent about your success.

Fear of Being Arrogant

Sometimes our guilt over success springs from fear of becoming arrogant. Maybe you've read one too many stories about the overnight success who suddenly starts acting like a diva, being rude to "the little people," and generally behaving as though she's better than everyone else. Or you may simply be worried that success will make you a less sympathetic, approachable, or down-to-earth person. People from communities who've faced prejudice and discrimination may have good reason to view success as an attribute of the very people who have kept their families down.

As in so many areas, women face a special obstacle in this regard. To become successful—whether in sports, entertainment, business, or the arts—you need a certain amount of self-confidence and entitlement. When you walk into a room, you've got to project the attitude that you belong there, that you've got something to offer, that you're the best possible person for the job. When you walk out onto the field, you've got to believe not only that you can win but also that you deserve to win, that winning is not a happy accident but what you do every day.

These are great attributes, and they're the key to success at the highest levels. But this conscious belief in your own worth is often exactly what women have been trained to avoid. What comes off as pleasant self-confidence in a man is often seen as self-absorbed, vain, or arrogant in a woman; what reads as natural male authority often translates into female bitchiness or pushiness. So for women in particular, it's important to distinguish between arrogance—based on a false sense of entitlement—and self-confidence—based on a true sense of worth.

Some of the suggestions I've made earlier can help in this regard: making sure to surround yourself with supportive friends
and loved ones; readjusting your identity; accepting conflict. I also
think it's useful to reconsider your attitudes about entitlement, arrogance, and self-confidence. Here are two suggestions for how to
clarify your thinking:

1. *Identify the behaviors you genuinely dislike—actions that imply entitlement and privilege.* Identify, too, the behaviors that indicate
   a genuine and appropriate self-confidence—actions that imply a clear understanding of what you're capable of and what
   you can expect. Then be rigorous with yourself about which
   actions you express. It's not okay to feel that you have the
   right to cut in front of a line because you're busier and more
   important than most people; if your newfound success is
   leading to that kind of arrogance, maybe you should question
   your sense of entitlement. On the other hand, it's perfectly
   okay to walk into a meeting and tell people without apology
   what you can do for them if they hire you—even to tell them
   that they're unlikely to find anyone else who's more qualified
   or better suited for the position. Cutting into a line says "I'm
   more deserving than you." Proclaiming your abilities says
   "I'm the right person for this job." Understanding the difference can help you avoid true arrogance while claiming your
   own success.

2. *Look to role models who express your own sense of how a successful person should behave.* This, again, is especially important
   for women: it's not easy finding women who wear their self-
   confidence easily. Too many female role models are media
   figures whose "nice girl" public personae mask their un-
   derlying ambition and drive, as though they just happened
   to fall into the highly coveted positions they occupy.
   Understanding this issue can motivate you to seek genuinely helpful role models who express confidence without

arrogance, and visualizing them can be an enormous source of strength.

If you'd like to work more on this key issue, consider the following exercise.

EXERCISE
Create an Arrogance Barometer

1. *Distinguish between arrogance and self-confidence.* Take a blank page and draw a line down the center, creating two columns. Label the left-hand column "Arrogant Behaviors." Label the right-hand column "Confident Behaviors."

2. *Identify arrogant and confident behaviors.* Working as quickly as you can, without giving yourself time to censor or filter your thoughts, list at least five behaviors under each column. More of either is okay, but make sure you list at least five of each. Set a timer and give yourself five minutes to complete the exercise.

3. *Evaluate your work.* When the timer goes off, take a minute to evaluate what you've written. Do you have a long list of arrogant behaviors and few or no confident behaviors? Are the items in both lists pretty much the same? Is there anything you would like to edit, change, or add?

4. *Complete your lists.* Work as long as you choose to complete your lists.

5. *Consolidate your thinking.* Write for at least five minutes on each of the following three questions:

     a. What is my biggest concern about being arrogant?

     b. What is my biggest concern about having self-confidence?

c. What is the true difference between arrogance and confidence?

6. *Practice acting from confidence.* The next day, choose one of the actions on your "Confident Behaviors" list. Commit to practicing that action at least once during your day. When you return home that night, write for at least five minutes about your experience. How did you feel? How did others react? What conclusion do you draw?

7. *Continue your practice.* If you feel this is a productive exercise for you, continue to practice the confident behaviors each day. You also might try adding new confident behaviors to your list, continuing to expand and deepen your idea of what confidence is and moving away from confusing it with arrogance.

8. *Avoid arrogant behaviors.* If you genuinely feel you have to struggle to refrain from arrogant behaviors, come up with a personal reward for each day you are arrogance-free and a selfless act for each time you catch yourself being arrogant. Your acts could include giving some money to a homeless person or a charity, going out of your way to be helpful to a stranger, letting someone go ahead of you in line, or any other consequence to remind yourself that your success does not entitle you to better treatment, only to the rewards of the success itself.

So far, we've considered how fears of failure, mediocrity, success, fear itself, and guilt can lead you to sabotage your own progress. Now it's time to consider another powerful emotion that many people would prefer to ignore: anger.

CHAPTER 6

Face Your Fear of Anger

I can't understand it," Joel said to me. "I've been training for years to get this chance. And now that I've finally got it, I'm going to blow it?"

My patient Joel had been playing hockey since he was five years old. Joel was a big, gentle guy with an easygoing smile and a quiet manner. Ever since he could remember, his father had woken him up at five in the morning and sent him out for skating practice. In high school, his father had set strict rules about dating so that Joel would have more time to devote to his training. Joel's college had been chosen with his hockey career in mind, and Joel's father had made sure that everything else took second place. Girls, studies, other interests, even vacation and holidays with the family all took a back seat to hockey.

Now, it seemed, Joel had finally become successful. After moving up steadily through the minor leagues, he had won a slot on a

major-league team and he'd been racking up a very decent record
for his first few games. His father was already talking about starting his own restaurant using Joel's soon-to-be-famous name.

Then, as so often happens, Joel went into a slump. But when he
came to me for help, I realized that here was a deeply angry man.
In my view, fear of his own anger against his father was a hidden
fear that Joel was unwilling to face.

"My father loves me," Joel insisted. "He only wants the best
for me." But the more we talked, the more Joel's anger emerged.
For years, Joel had felt that his father valued Joel only when he
succeeded, never when he played badly. The resentment that had
built up during those years was finally taking its toll.

For Joel, athletic success had become a double-edge sword. If
he did well, he had fulfilled his own goals for himself—but he
had also fulfilled his father's wishes for him. He'd become unable to tell the difference between pursuing his own dreams and
submitting to his father. Missing shots—avoiding the success he'd
worked so hard for—had become a kind of stand-in for independence. It was as if Joel were saying to his father, "I don't have to do
what *you* want. For once, I'm going to do what *I* want."

Yet it wasn't clear what Joel truly wanted. His goal was not to give
up his success or to lose games. Those were simply the only ways he
could see to say no to his powerful father and to express the anger
that had been building up all these years. That's why the missed
shots seemed so mysterious to Joel. He was deliberately, though unconsciously, trying to miss the net, driven by feelings of frustration,
helplessness, and anger that he wasn't willing to look at.

Joel had once had a dream in which he and his father were eating together and his father kept helping himself to food from Joel's
plate. Finally Joel took the plate and threw it on the floor. "Maybe
that was the only way you could stand up for yourself," I suggested when he related the dream to me. "But you should notice
that while you kept your father from taking advantage of you, you
didn't get to eat, either."

So for Joel, facing his hidden fears was crucial. Although Joel was able to admit that sometimes he got teed off at his father, he had trouble seeing how deep his anger went. His only way of expressing these feelings were his slump. His repeated failures on the ice were his way of saying, "This isn't working for me. There's something I need that I'm not getting."

For Joel to overcome his slump, he'd have to uncover these buried feelings. He'd need to distinguish between the kid who had—however unwillingly—to do whatever Dad told him, and the adult who now had the freedom to make his own choices. He'd have to decide what kind of relationship he wanted with his father now, and to figure out what kind of life Joel truly wanted for himself. At that point, if Joel wanted to give up hockey, stop training, or cut off all contact with his father, he would be choosing the life he truly wanted. Or perhaps he'd come to see that he had other options. Whatever he chose, it would be better than continuing to fail and ignoring his hidden fears.

The Language of Anger

To face our fear of anger, we first must become aware that we are angry. Joel had trouble recognizing this awareness—and perhaps you do, too. In our culture, women often have problems expressing or even experiencing their own anger, since we're all taught that nice girls don't get angry. Fear of being a bitch has kept many women from accessing their genuine anger.

On the other hand, now that powerful women have become more acceptable, we've fallen prey to another stereotype: the woman—or man—who is always angry, always making unreasonable demands or blowing up over little things. Ironically, both the person who is never angry and the one who seems always angry may be having an equally difficult relationship with their own anger. Both may be unwilling to look more specifically at just who they're angry at, and why.

Is fear of your own anger one of the fears you'd been hiding from yourself? Look at the following checklist to find out. Put a check mark in the box by any item that applies to you. Put an X by any item that really applies to you.

CHECKLIST
Am I Ignoring My Buried Anger?

☐ I frequently make stupid mistakes without understanding why.

☐ I'm often late.

☐ I often feel guilty.

☐ I often feel that I'm a bad person, sometimes without being able to say exactly why.

☐ I often blow up at little things.

☐ I often get very frustrated at little things.

☐ When I do get angry, I don't understand why the incident that set it off bothers me so much.

☐ I often become angry without expecting it; my anger simply catches me off guard.

☐ More than once, I've gotten angry with someone who I later realize didn't deserve it.

☐ In the past three months, I've had at least one blowup.

☐ Although I don't have blowups, I'm often afraid that I might.

☐ When other people express their anger, I find it deeply disturbing, even if they aren't angry with me.

- ☐ I drive recklessly, at least occasionally.

- ☐ I often get headaches or migraines.

- ☐ I often get stomachaches.

- ☐ I suffer from ulcers, colitis, or irritable bowel syndrome.

- ☐ I struggle with overeating, undereating, or binging and purging.

- ☐ I struggle with an addiction to drugs or alcohol.

- ☐ I never have a free minute—I'm always working.

- ☐ The people I know worry that I'm doing too much.

- ☐ I often feel anxious or worried about little things or for no reason at all.

- ☐ I often worry that others will be angry with me or that I've hurt their feelings.

- ☐ I frequently catch myself forgetting to do what I've promised in ways that cause trouble for other people.

- ☐ I often have accidents that hurt other people and/or their property—bumping into someone, spilling something on them, losing something I've borrowed, and so on.

- ☐ People frequently get annoyed at my jokes or teasing when I'm certain that I'm just kidding.

- ☐ When something upsets me, I often get very quiet and withdraw completely.

- ☐ My friends or loved ones have accused me more than once of pouting.

- ☐ I've found myself asking innocent questions that people seem to be offended or upset by.

- ☐ I often get so tired that I have to cancel plans that someone else has been looking forward to.

- ☐ I sometimes get into moods where everything that anyone says seems overly optimistic, irrelevant, or just plain silly.

- ☐ I often complain about little things—a person's ugly hairstyle, a missing report, a bad driver.

- ☐ I often feel critical of and annoyed with other people's stupidity, bad habits, or inconsiderate behavior.

- ☐ I often disagree strongly with people about things that don't really affect my own life, such as their political ideas, their eating habits, or their taste in movies.

- ☐ I often make fun of people or repeat critical gossip about them.

- ☐ I enjoy hearing people made fun of or gossiped about.

- ☐ I find myself frequently arguing with strangers such as clerks, people in line with me, or other drivers.

- ☐ I often fight with members of my family or with friends I'm close to.

- ☐ I generally believe that most people don't mean what they say.

- ☐ I generally think that most people can't be trusted.

- ☐ I feel that most groups are just out for what they can get.

- ☐ I believe that most people turn out to be phonies when you get to know them.

- ☐ I often feel that most people don't live up to my standards.

- ☐ I often feel that I myself don't live up to my own standards.

- ☐ I am frequently depressed.

- ☐ I often feel hopeless.

- ☐ I enjoy watching other people express their anger.

- ☐ I enjoy violent movies.

☐ I often find myself worrying about violent events.

☐ Certain issues, people, or memories can trigger an immediate angry response.

☐ I have the sense sometimes that others are afraid of my anger.

It's a long list, isn't it? That's because buried anger can take so many different forms and hide in so many different places. You may also have heard some types of buried anger referred to as *passive aggression*—expressing aggression while innocently proclaiming and perhaps even believing that one is not really angry.

Of course, not every item on this checklist is a foolproof sign of anger. Sometimes we make silly mistakes or misunderstand or show up late for reasons that have nothing to do with anger. Sometimes we really are too tired to keep an appointment; sometimes we really are just kidding! And we can certainly enjoy a brisk discussion or a contrary point of view without being guided by buried anger.

But if you felt especially disturbed by encountering any of these items or if you could feel the little bell going off in your brain that lets you know you've encountered something important, I urge you to take a closer look. Buried anger may well be the hidden emotion that's keeping you from wholeheartedly pursuing the life you want.

Don't Cut Off Your Nose to Spite Your Face

Whether our anger is buried or conscious, we need to understand that it isn't anger per se that's the problem—it's not being in control of how we express our anger. There are many situations in which we may feel anger and choose not to express it—against an unreasonable boss, for example, who isn't going to listen to us anyway, or against a parent who sometimes gets on our nerves but who we realize isn't going to change. Knowing that we feel angry and consciously deciding not to express our anger—or not expressing it to the person who provoked it—may be a very healthy choice.

The problem is when we do want to express our anger but fear doing so, either because we are worried about how the other person will react or because we don't want to admit our feelings. In such circumstances, our anger will often come out in some other way: against ourselves, other people, or even its true target. The long checklist suggests the many ways anger can be expressed covertly. Or we may, like Joel, start failing in areas where the target of our anger wants us to succeed.

Joel, for example, was using his missed shots and poor play as ways of expressing his anger against the father who seemed to value his success more than his love. Another patient, Petra, was so frustrated with the mother who insisted that she get married that she brought home one unacceptable boyfriend after another.

Although Joel and Petra succeeded in upsetting their parents, both had to deprive themselves to do so. Joel didn't really want to be failing in major-league hockey—he wanted either to leave the sport altogether or to succeed in it brilliantly. Petra didn't want to be dating a streak of loser guys—she wanted to be either happily single or happily married. But to punish their parents, both Joel and Petra were willing to sacrifice their own happiness, feeling that the only way to express their anger was to punish themselves—either to make their parents sorry or to keep them from getting what they wanted.

The colloquial expression for this behavior is "Cutting off your nose to spite your face." In my experience, we're most prone to engage in this kind of self-destructive aggression when we feel that we've been left virtually no control over our lives. Our parents—

or some other authority figure or loved one—seems to make all the rules and have all the power. In such a situation, the only thing you may be able to control is screwing up.

To me, cutting off your nose to spite your face is a negative use of anger. Yes, the person you're angry with may suffer—but you ultimately suffer more, often without even realizing what you're doing. Joel didn't know why he was stuck in a slump, any more than Petra realized why all the men she brought home were such poor choices for her. All they knew was that they felt small, helpless, frustrated, and angry. In fact, burying their anger, they didn't even know that. "I don't understand why I do these things," Petra would moan in her weekly sessions. "I don't understand what's happening to me," Joel would repeat, week after week. That sense of watching yourself act in ways you don't understand is one of the surest clues that you're dealing with a hidden fear, which quite often turns out to be anger.

SCIENCE MATTERS

The Biology of Anger

What happens to our bodies when we get angry? The biological reaction we experience is actually a primitive response that we developed eons ago in response to the possibility of danger. In fact, the biology of anger is remarkably similar to the biology of fear: both are aspects of the fight-or-flight response to a threat that we must either fight or run away from.

First, the hypothalamus, a region deep inside the brain, is stimulated by the perception of a threat. It stimulates the nervous system to constrict the arteries that carry blood to our skin, kidneys, and intestines. If we're about to fight or flee, we don't need to worry so much about digesting food. Nor do we want too much blood too close to the skin, in case we get wounded and bleed.

Meanwhile, the adrenal glands—located just above the kidneys—send a rush of adrenaline into our systems, which signals the arteries that carry blood to our muscles to open. Again, this makes sense: if we're facing a threat, we want our muscles to have as much energy as possible. At the same time, the stress hormone known as cortisol amplifies and prolongs adrenaline's effect, so that our bodies are up for a lengthy battle or a long flight.

Then, in response to the adrenaline rush, two other hormones enter our bloodstream: epinephrine and norepinephrine. These are our stimulation hormones: they respond to just about any type of stimulant or stressor, including anger, fear, heat, cold, pain, bleeding, burns, and physical exercise, as well as caffeine, nicotine, and alcohol. These two hormones make our hearts beat faster while further reducing the blood flow to our intestines and digestive systems. That's why anger, fear, and any other strong emotion—including falling in love—can make us feel alert, excited, ready to move, and up for a long bout of activity, even as it also decreases our appetite and makes it harder for us to digest our food.

The Positive Uses of Anger

"Okay," Joel said one day after we'd been meeting for a while. "I get that I'm cutting off my nose to spite my face, and I get that it's a negative use of anger. But I've already tried not to feel angry—and we see how well that's worked! What's my alternative?"

In my view, trying not to be angry is probably the least effective way of coping with our anger—just look back at the discussion of ironic processes in chapter 1 if you have any doubts! What is helpful is to recognize the positive uses of anger:

1. To regain control in a power struggle. ("If this must be a power struggle, I will win rather than you.")

2. To set a boundary. ("I will not be pushed past a certain point that I determine.")

3. To express your true feelings. ("I will speak out or act out my true emotions, wishes, and beliefs.")

4. To choose your true goals. ("I will do what I think is right for myself and not necessarily what you want me to do.")

5. To overcome feelings of hurt and powerlessness. ("Although you have hurt me, I will not sink down into that hurt feeling, but instead will rise up in anger.")

To me, these uses of anger have very positive effects when they're chosen consciously and expressed responsibly. This is the kind of anger that motivates battles against injustice, clarity in a confusing situation, assertion in the face of aggression. This is the kind of anger that says "I will do this because I know it's right," or "Don't tread on me," or "I will not be stopped." It's the kind of anger that helps us identify problems, reach our goals, mobilize our resources, set limits, and experience our own unique separate selves.

This is the kind of anger I'd like you to discover in yourself so you can bring your buried anger to the surface without fear—and then choose exactly what you want to do about it.

If you'd like to get to know your anger better, the following two exercises may help.

EXERCISE
Overcome Your Fear of Anger

1. *Relax.* Close your eyes and visualize descending the staircase to relax your body and clear your mind. As always, breathe and count on each step, counting down from eighteen.

2. *Visualize yourself in a place where you feel safe.* You might choose a real place or an imaginary one. As always, use sensory details—sight, hearing, smell, taste, and touch—to bring this place into focus and make it real for you. Spend some time— two or three minutes at least—enjoying this pleasant and absolutely safe environment.

3. *Leave your safe place to encounter someone with whom you are angry.* When you are ready, leave the safe environment you have imagined and move into a space where you encounter someone with whom you are angry. You can choose a person from your own life, or you can imagine someone you don't know, such as a clerk, who has sparked your anger.

4. *Use sensory detail to re-create the angry incident.* You can remember a real-life incident that actually upset you or imagine an incident that sparks your anger, such as feeling insulted by a clerk or being pushed by a stranger as you're crossing the street. As always, use details of sight, hearing, smell, taste, and touch to bring the incident to life.

5. *Allow yourself to get mad.* Whatever happened or would likely happen in real life, allow yourself to imagine yourself as angry. If you're not used to confronting your anger directly, you might find this an uncomfortable experience, but keep breathing and stay with it as long as you can. Remind yourself that anytime you like, you can return to the safe place from which you began. Meanwhile, observe as much as you can about how you behave and how the other person responds.

6. *Conclude the scene and return to your safe place.* When you're ready, allow the scene to end and return to the safe place you've imagined. Remain there for two or three minutes, or as long as you like, before you climb back up the stairs and open your eyes.

7. *Check in with your own body.* Having been angry, even if only briefly and in your imagination, how do you feel now? Is your

heart racing? Has your breathing quickened? What are you doing with your hands? How does your chest feel? Your stomach? Your throat? Notice your physical response to anger in detail as specific as you can make it.

8. *Identify your emotional response.* Ask yourself how you are feeling now. Do you still feel angry? Sad? Anxious? Relieved? Are you noticing that you feel happy? Powerful? Exhilarated? Or do you feel weak, regretful, guilty?

9. *Write about the experience.* Take at least five minutes to record how you feel and what you have learned. Be sure to note any thoughts, feelings, or images that float by—especially the "silly" ones! Don't judge or analyze; just record.

10. *Process your experience.* Consolidate your experience by answering the following questions:

    - When I got angry, what I noticed most in myself is _____
      _____.
    - What I noticed most in the other person was _____
      _____.
    - Before I got angry, I expected _____.
    - What actually happened was _____.
    - One possible reason for the gap between (or the similarity between) what I expected and what actually happened is
      _____.
    - When I get angry, one good thing that happens is _____
      _____.
    - When I get angry, one bad thing that happens is _____
      _____.
    - I could tip the balance further from bad to good by _____
      _____.
    - Next time I get angry, I want to _____.
    - With regard to anger, what I now most want to do is ___
      _____.

Listen to Your Anger

1. *Relax.* Close your eyes and relax your body by imagining your descent down a flight of eighteen stairs. As always, take a deep breath on every step, inhaling and exhaling as you count down from eighteen to one.

2. *Visualize yourself in a place where you feel safe.* You might choose a real place or an imaginary one. Feel free to use the same place you used in the previous exercise, or create an entirely new environment for yourself. As always, use sensory details—sight, hearing, smell, taste, and touch—to make your visualization as real as possible to you. Remain in this pleasant place for at least two or three minutes—longer if you like.

3. *Visualize your anger.* This is your opportunity to encounter your anger and learn what it's trying to tell you. Invite your anger into your safe place and visualize what enters. What color is your anger? What shape? Does it have a texture? Does it look like a person, an animal, an object, or some abstract image? Investigate your anger as thoroughly as possible, keeping it at whatever distance from yourself you find safe and comfortable, but allowing yourself to approach as needed to learn more.

4. *Invite your anger to speak to you.* In the scene you're imagining, picture yourself speaking to your anger. (If you're in a quiet, private place and you would rather speak aloud, feel free!) Tell your anger that you're aware that it's been trying to make itself heard and that you haven't wanted to give it that chance. Now you want to. What has your anger been trying to tell you? What does it want? What does it need you to hear?

5. *Listen to your anger.* Imagine what your anger might say. Allow it to speak without interruption or argument. If necessary, ask

more questions to encourage it or to clarify things for yourself. Make sure you're letting your anger tell you everything it wants to express.

6. *If you choose, respond.* You may want to tell your anger how you feel or what you think about what it's just said. If you're not ready to do that at this time, offer to reply at a later time.

7. *Thank your anger and conclude the scene.* Thank your anger for showing up and promise that you will always listen when it has something to say. In that way, it can express itself by speaking to you directly, rather than acting out or pushing you to behavior you don't consciously choose. Imagine your anger departing and give yourself a moment or two more to savor your safe and pleasant place before you climb the stairs (breathing and counting as you go) and open your eyes.

8. *Write about the experience.* To the best of your recollection, write down exactly what happened, focusing especially on exactly what your anger said to you and how you replied. Note as well how you feel and what you think about this experience. If you find yourself continuing the dialogue with your anger on paper, so much the better.

9. *Process your experience.* Consolidate your experience by answering the following questions:

    - One reason I haven't wanted to listen to my anger before is _____.
    - Something I've learned about my anger that I didn't know before is _____.
    - Now that I've heard from my anger, I resolve to _____ _____.
    - One way I can keep in touch with my anger rather than burying it is to _____.
    - When I next suspect that I have some buried anger inside, I will _____.

SCIENCE MATTERS

Making the Most of Our Stress Hormones

Like anger itself, our "anger hormones" are a double-edged sword. The epinephrine and norepinephrine that our body releases during anger or any other type of stress can have beneficial effects in small doses or for short periods: improved memory, sharper concentration, better performance. Martin Luther, by the way, once wrote that he liked to be a bit angry before he started one of his famous sermons; he thought the anger gave him a bit of an edge and brought out his best work, energizing him for the task ahead. Many of my athlete-patients feel the same way—a bit of anger brings out their best game.

But too much of these stimulating chemicals, and the balance starts to tip the other way: poor memory, decreased concentration, a decline in performance. Some people like to feel "psyched up" and a little nervous before a test, a presentation, a big game, or a performance: the stress hormones that flood their systems really do help them operate at their best levels. But too much anxiety, anger, or stress, however, and you go from smart to stupid, on edge to clumsy, sharp to dull.

Check it out for yourself. You're probably able to remember exactly what you said and did the last time you were only mildly annoyed. That's because the stress hormones sharpened your memory. But if you were really furious with someone, you're probably drawing a blank, because those very same hormones at a higher level were interfering with your memory.

So be careful. Like fire, anger serves you best when you're in control, not when it is.

Anger versus Aggression

As Joel unburied his anger, he experienced a wonderful thing: a renewed surge of the enthusiasm and joy he had once felt for his sport but that had been too long absent from his daily practices and his thrice-weekly games. "It's like hockey is really mine, for the first time in my life," he enthused. "Finally it's mine, and not my dad's."

Joel still has a lot of work to do on his relationship with his father. He's not sure how he feels about his father relying on him financially—starting the restaurant and profiting from Joel's career in other ways. He's not sure, either, how to process all the buried hurt and anger of the past twenty years. He knows that nothing would be served by blowing up at his dad or accusing him of all the wrongs Joel now feels he's committed; rather, Joel wants to set new limits with his father and let the past go. On the other hand, Joel isn't yet ready to put his old hurts and angers aside, and I don't necessarily think he should be. He'll need time to feel everything he's been burying all these years, and then more time to decide what he wants to do about it.

Meanwhile, though, Joel has at least reversed the slump in his game and is back at the top of his form. Having rediscovered his joy in hockey, he's able to play for himself, sure in the knowledge that he's pursuing his own dreams, his own vision of a life that's right for him.

Part of Joel's transformation came when he grasped the difference between aggression and assertion. Aggression is the desire to hurt or control others. Assertion is the intention to set limits and to express one's own feelings. Two assertive people can agree to disagree, reach a compromise, or work out their differences, because both of them want a situation in which everybody wins. An aggressive person, though, won't feel that he or she has actually won unless somebody else also loses. Joel is looking for ways to assert himself with his father in ways that aren't defined by making his father pay or doing to him what he did to Joel. Instead, he's trying to get in touch with his own inner sense of right and wrong, his own desire for fulfilling his dreams and living a good life.

In this journey, he's found great comfort in the centuries-old words of Rabbi Hillel; I think the words sum up the distinction perfectly:

> If I am not for myself, who will be for me?
>
> If I am only for myself, what am I?
>
> And if not now, when?

In this chapter, we've explored how hidden fears of anger can interfere with getting the life we want. We're now ready to move on to our next chapter, where we'll look at other hidden fears: fears of envy and isolation.

CHAPTER 7

Conquer Your Fears of Envy and Isolation

My patient Sonora was in distress. An aspiring actress, she had just been offered a significant role on the spin-off of a very successful TV series. Although nothing in show business is certain, it seemed as though Sonora was finally about to achieve the standing she'd always dreamed of. She should have been on top of the world. Instead, she was paralyzed by anxiety.

Sonora had found herself so upset by the offer that she'd called me to schedule an emergency session. When she arrived at my office, disheveled and tear-stained, she managed to give me a rueful smile. "I don't understand it," she said to me as we sat down. "I've been a complete basket case all morning. But I can't figure out why."

As I had done with Paul, who seemed so upset at the prospect of becoming partner in his law firm, I asked Sonora to tell me what she thought her new, successful life might be like. She quickly made it clear that she thought professional success would condemn her to personal isolation.

"If I really make it, I won't have anyone to talk to," she told me. "Even if my old acting buddies are nice about it, what are we going to do—go out to the restaurants they can afford, or the ones I can afford? How can I have them over to an apartment that's ten times more expensive than what they can afford? How can they not always be wondering when I'll introduce them to my agent or get them an interview with a casting director? Everyone will want something from me—no one will be honest with me, and even if they are, I won't know if they're flattering me or just putting me down to be mean, or . . . The only people I'll ever be able to trust will be people at my new level—and how will I know whether they really value me or are just dazzled, too, by my success?"

"So you're afraid of being isolated," I responded.

Sonora nodded vigorously. "I'll still want to be friends with my old friends—but they won't," she said.

"Why not?" I asked.

"Because they'll all think I'm so stuck up!" Sonora blurted out. "They'll think I think I'm better than they are!"

"Do you think you're better than they are?" I asked.

"What difference does it make what I think?" Sonora said angrily. "Everyone will be talking about who I slept with to get this part, or how I'm all technique and no soul, or how I'm all looks and no talent. Or else they'll start tearing me down, you know, 'She's getting so fat lately,' or 'I can't believe they didn't notice those bags under her eyes,' or—whatever! Nobody's going to give me any credit for anything at all. They'll all think it should have been them—and maybe it should have been, but . . . " Her flow of words sputtered to a halt and she stared at me, torn between anger and tears.

"It sounds as though you think your friends will be envious of you," I suggested, and she laughed.

"You can say that but I can't," she said bitterly. "If I say they're envious, they'll just look at me, like, 'Why in the world would I be envious of you?' And you know what the worst of it is? I've done exactly the same thing. I've dropped people because they got a part I wanted or because they were jetting out to L.A. during pilot season. I've said all those nasty, bitchy things behind my friends' backs about why it should have been me instead of them. I've done every single one of those things that I now think they're going to do to me. And if you'd told me I was being envious, I wouldn't have believed you. But I see it now."

Sonora had hit upon one of the most painful aspects of the fear of envy. Of all the seven deadly sins, envy seems the hardest to come to terms with. Most people will admit to lust, greed, sloth, pride, even anger and gluttony, long before they face up to envy, whether their own or that of others.

Even when a person is willing to face her hidden fears and admit her fear of envy, she worries that acknowledging this fear will make her sound arrogant. Who is she to think other people envy her? Why would she assume she's so far above them as to provoke envy? Doesn't she think that the people in her life have better things to do than to tear her down? Perhaps it's her own arrogance that's the problem and not their envy.

Worse, to talk about this fear might cause the people who envy her to become even angrier and more disapproving. Besides being angry about her success, they'll be angry at being called envious. To admit to envy is to admit that there's something you want in your own life that you're not getting, and that raises all sorts of fears: that you're not good enough or that you want something you feel guilty about wanting. And maybe you're also afraid of getting what you want and provoking other people's envy. So often, neither the envied nor the envious want to look at what's really going on.

Still, being honest about the situation gives us a chance to find out what we might actually do about it. So let's take a deep breath and look more closely at the fear of envy.

Envy and Isolation

Sonora's concerns revealed one of the most painful aspects of fearing envy: the fear of isolation. When we envy another person, we feel like the perpetual outsider, nose pressed up against the bakery window, longing for something we believe we can't have. We're also lonely when we are envied, the target of anger, frustration, and rejection—often by the people whom we count on most.

And yet envy seems to be an integral part of the human personality, a primal emotion that has its roots in infancy. One of the earliest scientific accounts of envy was written in 1877 by evolutionary theorist Charles Darwin, who kept a detailed record of his observations while taking care of his infant son. Though the boy was only fifteen months old, Darwin noted that "jealousy was plainly exhibited when I fondled a large doll." Even before he could talk, Darwin's son seemed to envy the doll—which he probably mistook for a child getting the fatherly affection that he, at that moment, was not. So perhaps the link between fear of envy and fear of isolation has its roots in our infant experience: watching our parents care for another child, we worry that we'll be isolated, left out from a parent-child bond that sometimes seems so deep that there's room for only two. And if we are the child being cared for, we can perhaps feel very early on the anger and resentment from the siblings or other family members who feel that we're getting love that is rightfully theirs.

Significantly, infants seem able to distinguish between parents turning away to focus on another interest and parents turning away to focus on another child. A 1998 study by researchers from the University of Miami School of Medicine and Laval University in Québec found that while infants didn't like being temporarily ignored while their mothers looked at a book, they liked even less being ignored while their mothers played with an infant-sized doll. Like Darwin's son, they seemed jealous of the doll, envying the attention their mothers gave it. And while experts had long been inclined to put the first emergence of envy at eighteen months, this groundbreaking study discovered envy among children who were even younger.

Psychologist Sybil Hart and her colleagues put seventy-six twelve-month-old infants in four different situations in which their mothers and a female stranger directed positive attention toward a doll or a picture book while temporarily ignoring the infant. The mothers and the stranger engaged in a series of sixty-second segments, sometimes merely speaking with one another, sometimes looking at a book, sometimes cooing over a doll as though it were a child. Sometimes the stranger held the book or doll, sometimes the mother did. The infants had been playing happily on the activity quilt. How would they respond when their mother took her attention elsewhere, even for as short a time as sixty seconds?

Generally, they didn't like it. They made "negative vocalizations"—little cries of protest—and tried to get their mothers to notice them, especially when the mothers were holding another object and most especially when that object was a doll. Although the infants had seemed content to play alongside their mothers before the doll was introduced, now they interrupted that play and directed their attention to what the grown-ups were doing. They also tended to ignore the doll, though they were likely to touch or reach for the book.

In other words, when their mothers were simply ignoring them—talking with a stranger, looking at a book—the children tried to get in on whatever Mommy was doing. But when their mothers seemed to be paying attention to another child, the children tried to get Mommy to pay attention to them. The children didn't seem to like it when their mother's attention was turned elsewhere, but their feelings seemed far stronger when envy of another "child" was involved.

It's always risky to interpret what an infant is feeling, and the researchers called for further study to learn more. But their results seemed to indicate that even a one-year-old child feels the pain of being left out.

Isolation Hurts

Sonora felt that pain, too, and she seemed unable to enjoy or even to tolerate her success for fear that it might lead to further isolation. Indeed, when I asked Sonora why she minded losing the friendship of people whom she was portraying as envious and small-minded, she looked at me as though I were crazy.

"But they're my friends," she said, once again torn between anger and tears. "They're the ones who've been there for me when I wasn't making it. They're the ones who know what it's like. They're the ones who understand." She smiled bitterly. "Of course, if I make it and they don't, I'll have a whole new set of problems, and they probably won't understand that. How could they? They'll think that someone who's on top of the world like I will be can't have any problems at all. They'll all be sitting around together, talking about how hard it is—and how can I be part of that?"

Sonora's pain at being excluded has not only an emotional basis but also a biological one. Experiments conducted by scientists from UCLA and Macquairie University in Sydney, Australia, revealed that both physical pain and the pain of social rejection seem to activate the same areas of the brain. In an extraordinary set of experiments that culminated in 2006, psychologist Naomi I. Eisenberger and her colleagues revealed that physical and emotional pain are extremely similar—perhaps even identical.

Eisenberger and her team approached the problem in more than one way, but the most fascinating of her experiments to me is the one she conducted in 2006. In that study, Eisenberger and her UCLA colleagues asked several dozen female students to take part in an experiment they were told was to measure the impact of physical discomfort in people's daily lives. As is so often the case with psychological studies, participants didn't know that the experimenters were really trying to measure something else—in this case, the pain of social isolation.

Accordingly, students were simply told that they'd be subject to an uncomfortable sensation from a heat delivery device. They were given a sample "stimulus"—an unpleasant burst of heat—and shown how to use the "pain unpleasantness rating scale" to indicate their levels of discomfort. They were told that first, researchers would take a baseline sample of their responses to the device; then they'd play a game of cyberball—a virtual ball-tossing game conducted over the Internet with two other people at different laboratories; and then, during the final thirty seconds of the game, they'd be given three more mildly unpleasant stimuli.

Participants believed that their job was to rate the stimuli. What they didn't realize was that researchers were also interested in their experience of playing cyberball, which was actually a computer simulation that didn't involve other people at all, but only cartoons on a screen. The cyberball game was designed to expose participants to one of three conditions:

1. Social inclusion, in which all three "players" apparently tossed the ball around together.

2. Noninclusion, in which the experimental subject was told that due to "technical difficulties" with the "Internet hookup," she could watch the other players but not join in.

3. Overt exclusion, in which the subject seemed to be playing with two other people for about fifty seconds but then was excluded for about a hundred seconds when the other "players" apparently stopped throwing her the ball.

In all three cases, participants got three "heat stimuli" toward the end of the game, at a threshold they had previously rated as "very unpleasant."

Immediately afterward, participants were given a test to measure their social distress. To continue with the original cover story, they were also asked how distracting they'd found it to be zapped with the heat device. Next, they were given a questionnaire designed to measure their psychological health, so researchers could factor in participants' own sensitivity to anxiety or stress. Finally, the researchers came clean and explained the true nature of the study. Then they went off to tally their results.

What they found was that being left out of the game—either because of "technical difficulties" or because two other "players" had supposedly ignored them—was extremely distressing to participants, so that those who were excluded—for either reason—reported more sensitivity to physical pain. This was as expected because of the results of Eisenberger's previous study that had discovered that the same areas of the brain that are active during physical pain—the anterior cingulate cortex and the right ventral prefrontal cortex—are active during social exclusion as well. Being left out hurts—literally—and everyone who fears the isolation that results from being envied knows it.

Who's Responsible?

One of the hardest aspects of these fears—of envy and of isolation—is feeling that you are somehow responsible for your own pain. Recall my patient Teresa, the tennis pro, who feared that becoming a champion would cost her the companionship of her rivals on the circuit. Teresa was so unwilling to look at the conflict between her fears of isolation and her dreams of victory that she developed a series of increasingly major injuries. On some level, she wanted the problem to be taken out of her hands: if she was injured, she couldn't play, and then she wouldn't have to choose.

Her story was similar to that of Andrea Jaeger, who in 1981 at the age of sixteen was the world's second-ranked tennis player, but who left the game to become an Episcopal nun. Jaeger had come from an abusive family, and her friendship with her fellow athletes was particularly important to her as well. As she explained to the *Times* of London in early 2007, playing in tournaments was agony:

"I was sitting in my hotel room all night going, 'Well, everybody thinks I'm great because I won, but what about the person I beat? How's she feeling?' I was tormented."

Jaeger's crucial moment came in 1983, when her father threw her out of their rented London house during the Wimbledon finals. Jaeger couldn't think of anywhere else to go but the house of her opponent and neighbor Martina Navratilova, who took her in. The next day, Jaeger let her friend win the match in a mere fifty-four minutes. "I never could have looked in the mirror if I went out and tried my heart out and won," Jaeger says, describing the problem as a moral issue. But I think it was also a psychological one: Jaeger had needed Navratilova's help when her own father had rejected her. It must have seemed unbearable to risk losing yet another attachment.

Like Teresa, Jaeger "resolved" the conflict by becoming injured, in her case a shoulder injury that caused her to leave tennis permanently. Although Jaeger sees the injury in religious terms—God taking away her gift—I'm again more inclined to view it psychologically, as a way of avoiding her hidden fears. "When I was injured, to be honest, I was relieved," Jaeger told the *Times*. "I thought, 'Finally I can go and be me.'"

Apparently for Jaeger, being herself meant not being envied, not competing with her friends, not being valued for her victories on the court. But for Teresa and for Sonora, giving up their calling didn't seem like an option. Although Teresa didn't want to lose her friends, she loved playing, and she loved striving for ever higher levels of play. Likewise, Sonora had wanted to be an actress her entire life, and despite the envy and isolation she feared, she found the prospect of the TV role thrilling.

Teresa's injuries and Sonora's anxiety attack were each ways of avoiding the painful prospect that they might be forced to choose between fulfilling their dreams and losing their friends. In my view, however, they had other options that they might explore as soon as they were willing to attend to their own hidden fears.

Although envy—our own and others'—may be a primal part of life, it's also a part of life we can cope with. We may not be able to prevent others from envying us, we may not even be able to stop fearing that they might, but we can find more effective ways of living with that fear.

Revising Your Identity

If you're feeling hamstrung by the fear of envy, one step you may find useful is to readjust your identity, transforming your self-concept from "failure" to "success." Sometimes we hold on to early ideas about who we are and then feel guilty, anxious, or confused about the gap between those ideas and our new reality. To pursue the life we really want, we need to revise our vision of who we really are.

A classic example is the formerly heavy woman who loses a lot of weight. She looks great and feels great, but she also faces a profound shift in both her own identity and in the relationships she has with others. From being the "safe" friend who wasn't particularly attractive, she may have become the threat either to her other heavy friends, who envy her new thinness, or to her more traditionally attractive friends, who were used to seeing her as below them in looks and sexual appeal. Her new, more attractive self provokes an envy she isn't used to, even as she also has to figure out a new relationship to her own sexuality and physical presence.

This can be challenging, and sometimes it's easier to wish for the old days when she knew exactly who she was and what to expect from her friends. But if she is willing to accept that her new achievements have created a new identity, she can look more clearly at the relationships she has and decide how she feels about them. She can decide who really loves her despite any momentary envy they may feel and despite who needs her to stay stuck in her old unhappy state. She can find ways to encourage her friends to accept her new identity and to set boundaries on how their envy affects her. She can keep, discard, and transform her current relationships, and she can create new relationships based on her new sense of herself. Before she can work with her friends' envy, however, she has to shift her own identity, seeing herself as she is now and not as she's always been.

Likewise, as Teresa and Sonora moved into their more successful incarnations, they had to readjust their identities. Before they could consider their relationships to others, they had to rework their relationship to themselves. Teresa had to see herself not as a lonely, isolated teenager who was living out a schedule her parents had created for her, but as a self-possessed, actualized young woman who was pursuing a dream she herself had chosen. Sonora had to let go of the frustrated, dissatisfied actress who bonded with others on the grounds of mutual disappointment, and imagine herself as an empowered performer surrounded by people who appreciated and encouraged any success she was lucky enough to achieve. Reworking their identities was the first step in refashioning their relationships—deciding whom they still wanted to be close to and what their friendships would now be like.

If you think that you, too, would benefit from rethinking your identity, fill out the following questionnaire. As always, I suggest beginning with quick, impulsive answers and then returning for longer and more thoughtful replies. Remember, there are no right or wrong answers—this is about self-exploration, not about "getting it right." Remember, too, that the "success" or "failure" you'll consider may be in any or all domains: love, marriage, family, friendships, career, life's work, money, or some other area of your personal or public life. Choose whatever areas in your life feel most urgent to you.

QUESTIONNAIRE
*How Am I Defined by Failure? How
Am I Defined by Success?*

1. Picture yourself at a point in your life where things are not
   going well for you. You may choose the present time or sometime in the past. Try to pick the time you have the strongest
   emotions about, a time that you feel has helped to shape your
   identity. Answer the following questions from the point of
   view of that person:

   a. Who are you? Describe yourself in a single sentence,
      ideally twenty-five words or less: _____
      _____.

   b. If someone were to meet you for only a moment or
      two, what he or she would notice about you would be
      _____.

   c. What he or she would likely miss about you would be
      _____.

   d. Imagine that someone is spending the day with you,
      in the domain you're considering. If you're thinking of
      work issues, imagine that it's a day of work. If you're
      thinking about romance, imagine that it's a day-long
      date or romantic encounter. Having spent a day with
      you in this area where you feel frustrated, what the
      person would learn about you is _____
      _____.

   e. What he or she would likely miss about you would be
      _____.

   f. How do you feel about how you are seen? _____
      _____.

g. What might you do to feel better about how you are seen? Or, if you are perfectly happy with the impression you make, what do you do that you feel works well for you? _____

_____.

h. Your greatest strength in the area you're considering is

_____.

i. Your greatest weakness in the area you're considering is _____.

j. Your most important goal is to _____

_____.

k. The thing you want most to avoid is _____

_____.

l. Those loved ones who know you best see you as _____

_____

_____.

m. Most of your relationships are based on _____

_____.

n. What you get from your relationships that you appreciate is _____

_____.

o. What you'd like from your relationships that you're not getting is _____

_____.

p. What your loved ones most appreciate getting from you is _____

_____.

q. What they'd like from you that they're not getting is

_____.

   r. How do you feel about the relationships you have
      now? _____.

   s. How do you feel about the life you have now? _____

      _____.

   t. What could you do to make your life more the way you
      want it to be? _____

      _____.

2. Now picture yourself at a point in your life where you have achieved what you define as success. Again, you may choose the present time or sometime in the future. Try to pick the time you have the strongest emotions about, a time you feel represents the fulfillment of the most important goals you have been working for. Answer the following questions from the point of view of that person:

   a. Who are you? Describe yourself in a single sentence,
      ideally twenty-five words or less: _____

      _____.

   b. If someone were to meet you for only a moment or
      two, what he or she would notice about you would be

      _____.

   c. What he or she would likely miss about you would be

      _____.

   d. Imagine that someone is spending the day with you,
      in the domain where you've achieved your new success. Having spent a day with you in this area where
      you now feel successful, what the person would learn
      about you is _____

      _____.

   e. What he or she would likely miss about you would be

      _____.

f. How do you feel about how you are seen? _____
_____.

g. What might you do to feel better about how you are seen? Or, if you are perfectly happy with the impression you make, what do you do that you feel works well for you? _____
_____.

h. Your greatest strength in the area you're considering is
_____.

i. Your greatest weakness in the area you're considering is _____.

j. Your most important goal is to _____
_____.

k. The thing you want most to avoid is _____
_____.

l. Those loved ones who know you best see you as _____
_____.

m. Most of your relationships are based on _____
_____.

n. What you get from your relationships that you appreciate is _____
_____.

o. What you'd like from your relationships that you're not getting is _____
_____.

p. What your loved ones most appreciate getting from you is _____.

q. What they'd like from you that they're not getting is
_____.

r. How do you feel about the relationships you have now?
_____

s. How do you feel about the life you have now? _____
_____

t. What could you do to make your life more the way you want it to be? _____
_____

3. Now that you've filled out the parts of questions 1 and 2, check in with yourself by answering the following questions:

a. How do you feel right now? Anxious? Exhilarated? Sad? Angry? All of the above? None of the above? Numb? Confused? Describe your emotional state as accurately and specifically as you can. Remember, there are no right or wrong answers. Just tell yourself how you feel. _____
_____

b. How do you feel physically? Check in with your body, allowing your awareness to move slowly down from the crown of your head through your face, neck, throat, chest, torso, stomach, groin, hips, legs, and toes. What is your body telling you? _____
_____

c. Suppose that a person you trust completely—a loved one, teacher, guide, or spiritual figure—were with you now, reading your responses and empathizing with your emotional state. What advice would he or she give you? _____
_____

d. What surprised you most about this experience? _____
_____

e. What upset you most? _____

_____

f. What excited or pleased you most? _____

_____

g. Write for at least five minutes about your responses,
to complete this questionnaire. You can do this in the
form of a conversation with the guide you invoked
earlier, as a regular journal entry, or in any other form
that feels like a helpful way to process your experience.

Learning to Accept Conflict

Another key aspect of coping with our fear of envy is learning
to accept conflict. Although many of our loved ones may not feel
envious of our success, it's entirely possible that many will. Sometimes this envy is a passing phase or a relatively small part of the
relationship; sometimes it characterizes the relationship almost
entirely. Either way, accepting that we may sometimes displease
or distress the people we love is crucial to our ability to wholeheartedly pursue the life we want. Fear of envy can only have so
much power over us if we're not looking at it. Seeing it clearly
means accepting conflicts, even if we don't like them.

This kind of acceptance is especially tough for women, who
are generally socialized to feel that they have to please everybody. Becoming more successful—personally, professionally, romantically—may indeed turn some people off, threaten some old
friends, alienate some new ones.

When I pointed this out to Sonora, she looked at me in horror. "But I thought therapy was about learning to get along with
people," she said. "You know—doing it right."

"So you think that if you do everything right, no one will ever envy you?" I asked.

"I don't know," Sonora said slowly. Clearly, she had never thought of it this way before. "I guess I hoped I could manage that."

"Let's say for the moment that you can't—that no matter what you do, some of your friends are likely to feel envious of you, just as in the past you have felt envious of the more successful people you knew. Can you consider the possibility that it's not in your power to control their envy?"

"All right," Sonora said even more slowly.

"All right," I repeated. "Then—so what?"

"What?"

"So what? What difference does it make to you that someone else is envious? Why does that matter to you at all?"

Sonora considered this for several minutes, and we returned to the topic many, many times over the course of our work together. Ultimately Sonora had to decide whether she was more interested in keeping the good opinion of people who envied her—basically because of their dissatisfaction with their own lives—or in becoming the fully realized, joyous person she had it in her to be. Eventually she became more willing to accept that others might not always respond the way she'd prefer, which brought her a certain amount of sorrow and frustration, but which also empowered her to take bigger risks and freed her to enjoy her own success.

If you'd like to work on accepting the presence of envy and on strengthening your own responses to it, try the following exercise. As with other exercises in this book, it relies on the power of visualization and the reconsolidation of memory to help transform your ability to respond. (For more on the scientific basis for the effectiveness of visualization, see pages 26 and 116. For more on how the reconsolidation of memory can help you respond more effectively, see pages 69–70.)

EXERCISE
Challenge Your Fear of Envy

1. *Relax.* Use deep breathing to relax your body and clear your mind. As always, see yourself descending a flight of eighteen stairs, breathing and counting backward as you go.

2. *Visualize a situation in which you are envied.* Imagine a situation in which you are confronting the envy of someone you care about. As you have done in previous exercises, use specific sensory details—from sight, hearing, smell, taste, and sensation—to bring the situation into focus and allow your emotions to arise.

3. *Visualize the envy itself.* See the other person's envy literally floating out of his or her body and coming to rest between you. See this envy as specifically as possible. What shape is it? What color? Does it have a smell? Is it moving or changing, or does it seem fixed and solid? Does it look like a person, animal, or object you recognize? Take some time to respond to the envy in the room with each of your five senses.

4. *Create a shield to keep this envy at a safe distance.* Accept the other person's envy in this instance, but choose the distance at which you would like it to remain. Then visualize some kind of protective device to maintain that distance—a piece of armor, a wall of light, a strong wind, or some other type of shield, anything to keep the envy as far away from you as you choose.

5. *Continue your activity in the scene.* Whatever you were doing when the other person's envy materialized, continue—and notice how the envy responds. Commit to maintaining the distance you have chosen and remember that it's in your power to do so. If necessary, experiment with different ways to maintain the distance you have chosen. Notice your own response as well.

6. *Conclude the scene.* When you are ready, find a way to end the scene you are imagining. Return to your actual surroundings by ascending the stairs, breathing and counting up from one to eighteen.

7. *Check in with your body.* Notice how you are feeling now.

8. *Write about the experience.* As always, take at least five minutes to process what you've learned.

The Dangers of Isolation

Sometimes isolation isn't the result of envy per se, but rather the result of becoming unlike those we once knew and felt close to. Your family, friends, and community may not envy you, but you feel that you've lost much of the basis of your connection. Suppose you are the only woman from your college group of friends to go to medical school, or the only man from your neighborhood to play the violin. You're suddenly facing pressures, demands, options, and rewards that the people you once counted on may not understand. They may not envy you; they may even look down on you ("She's a terrible mother—busy all the time"; "What kind of man plays music like that?"). Or they may be genuinely pleased for you ("We're all so proud of Terry! She is the only one of us who's ever done anything like this!"). Either way, your success has to some extent separated you from people you once felt close to. That can be a painful situation. Indeed, as research by Jean M. Twenge and her colleagues has shown, it can lead to self-defeating behavior without your realizing why.

Twenge's intriguing study "Social Exclusion Causes Self-Defeating Behavior" was designed to test the assumption that "the need to belong is one of the most basic and fundamental human motivations." She and fellow researchers Kathleen R. Catanese and Roy F. Baumeister wondered whether people who felt that they didn't belong would engage in such self-defeating behaviors as making irrational financial choices, eating unhealthy food, avoiding exercise, and procrastinating. So they recruited a number of college students to take a bogus personality test that in reality measured nothing at all but that the students believed would give them information about their future prospects. Some students were told that their results indicated a rich network of social relationships that would continue throughout their lives. Others were told that they would likely end up alone for most of their adult lives. Still others were told that they'd have good relationships but that they were accident-prone and would face more difficulties than other people. The researchers wanted to make sure they were seeing the results of fearing isolation and not simply unhappiness or difficulty.

Of course, when the experiment was over, the students got a full explanation of what had happened and were assured that the personality test they had taken measured nothing at all; the results were randomly assigned and the test results hadn't even been scored. Meanwhile, though, three groups of students had imagined three futures for themselves: relationship-rich; isolated; and relationship-rich but unlucky.

The first group of fifty undergraduates were given the test, told their results, and then asked to rate their moods. Then they were given the choice of participating in two lotteries. If they won the lottery, they'd get a financial prize. If they lost, they'd have to listen to a three-minute tape of fingernails scraping along a blackboard. Lottery A offered a 70 percent chance of winning $2 and a 30 percent chance of having to hear the noise. Lottery B offered a 2 percent chance of winning $25 and a 98 percent chance of having to hear the noise.

Clearly, the more rational choice was Lottery A. Yet participants who had been told they would end up isolated were far more likely to choose Lottery B—even more likely to do so than participants who had been told they'd end up in relationships but unlucky. In fact, only 6 percent of those who believed they'd end up in good relationships chose Lottery B, while 21 percent of the "unlucky" group did—and 60 percent of the "future alone" group. Think about it: fifty undergraduate students, all from the same university, making such wildly different choices just based on the expectation of whether they could expect connection or had to fear isolation.

What makes these results even more remarkable is that the mood tests the students took didn't reveal any significant differences in mood between the unlucky or alone groups. Understandably, both groups felt much worse than the group for whom a happier future had been predicted, but the alone group didn't rate their moods as worse than the related but unlucky group. Yet the alone group chose the less rational financial option almost three times as often as the related but unlucky group. Clearly, their sense of isolation was driving them to make more self-defeating choices, even though they weren't aware of feeling worse than people who had been given other types of bad news.

A second experiment reinforced the conclusion that isolation can be a powerful predictor of self-defeating behavior. In that procedure, the students were again given their bogus test results and were then given three health-related choices: between a candy bar and a low-fat granola bar; between getting important information about their health and reading magazines; and between exercise and resting. People who thought they'd have rich relationship networks—whether they expected to be lucky or unlucky—were twice as likely to choose healthy behaviors as did students who believed they'd end up alone. And again, these results didn't correlate to students' self-reported moods after hearing their test results. Believing they were doomed to isolation seemed the only significant factor leading to the self-defeating behavior.

A final experiment measured the likelihood of procrastination. In addition to the bogus personality test, participants were told that they'd be given a test of "nonverbal intelligence." They were also told that practicing some math equations for ten or fifteen minutes would significantly improve their performance on the test. Then they were left alone with practice materials, a Tetris Game Boy, and a bunch of popular magazines, including *Wired*, *Cosmopolitan*, and *Maxim*. Sure enough, the students who believed they'd end up in rich relationships—whether or not they also thought they'd have "unlucky" lives—were far more likely to use their time studying than those who believed they'd end up alone. And again, mood wasn't a factor. The fear of isolation seemed to trump all other fears, at least where self-defeating behavior was concerned. "Apparently," wrote the researchers, "social exclusion can increase self-defeating behavior without emotion playing a substantial part."

In other words, believing that you don't belong—or eventually won't belong—profoundly affects the choices you make, even if you're not experiencing yourself as unhappy, angry, or scared. Even if you do experience these emotions, feeling them in response to another problem—in the experiment, fear of facing accidents and other misfortunes—affects your behavior quite differently than when they're produced by fear of isolation.

When I read this study, I felt I understood much better why Teresa—and Andrea Jaeger—suffered their injuries; why Sonora was disabled by a panic attack on what should have been one of the happiest days of her life. Such self-sabotaging behaviors seemed to promise an end to their isolation, the possibility that they'd be restored to the groups to which they had once belonged. Even more than fear of envy per se, fear of isolation seems to be one of the most powerful hidden forces in our lives.

Creating a Winner's Circle

What's the solution? How do we pursue the success we desire—in love, family, work, and personal life—without paying a terrible price for the isolation we fear? How do we keep our relationships intact while striving for the best of which we're capable? How do we attend to these hidden fears without succumbing to despair and self-sabotage?

Alas, there are no easy answers to these questions. Sometimes the choices we face include the prospect of more isolation than we'd like. Sometimes we are in situations where it's hard to find intimates, companions, and people with whom we can share what's most important to us. Sonora might have been in for a lonely time as she moved from being a struggling actress to a more successful one; Teresa might indeed have trouble maintaining friendships either with her rivals on the course or with nonathletes off the court. Anyone who chooses a unique path, who marches to the measure of her own drummer, risks some time—maybe even a lot of time—alone.

However, facing your choices honestly and then making the best decision possible under the circumstances is vastly preferable to self-sabotaging behavior. As I think of Andrea Jaeger, for example, I wonder what she would have chosen had she been able to identify and face her hidden fears. Perhaps she would have left the sport anyway—but voluntarily, not as the result of an injury she felt she had no control over. Or perhaps she would have found a way to bond with her fellow athletes even while going all out to beat them on the court. (Clearly, Martina Navratilova saw no contradiction between helping a competitor privately and defeating her publicly!) Perhaps Jaeger would have channeled her love of tennis into teaching or coaching; or perhaps she would have found some other solution to her dilemma. By ignoring her fear of isolation and hoping that her problems would somehow resolve themselves, she ended up solving her problems covertly, through injury, rather than through a free and open choice.

Teresa was luckier. Because she was working so hard in therapy to understand her true motives, dreams, and desires, and because she was willing to confront her fears, she realized that the solution for her lay in trying to establish a network of friends and a supportive romantic relationship outside the sport she loved so much. Unlike Navratilova, she couldn't handle bonding with her rivals one minute and trying to defeat them the next—but she could try to make friends in other contexts and to build a romantic partnership with a man who wasn't going to compete with her.

Sonora likewise decided that her acting meant too much to her to hold back simply for the sake of friends struggling with their own career frustrations. She committed to being as open and clear as possible with every one of her old friends, so that those relationships that could survive her new status, would. She prepared herself to let go of any relationships that seemed overly marked by envy or shared misery. And she accepted the possibility that her new success might in any case be short-lived and that the ups and downs of show business might not always go her way.

"I really want friends I can count on through both the good times and the bad," Sonora told me. "It's going to be challenging—but I can see that being honest, with them and with myself, is the key."

What about you? What kinds of relationships are in your life, and how do they help you overcome your own fears of isolation? Do you mainly know people who support you, or who tear you down? Have you surrounded yourself with a cheering section, or are you constantly having to defend yourself against insults, putdowns, and guilt trips? Thinking about your social and personal circle may help you make different choices about whom you want to be close to—or it may help you realize that your current friends and loved ones are actually happy to give you all the support you need.

The following exercise can help you think about these issues more clearly. And for those times when isolation just seems to be the order of the day, I've offered some further suggestions for making healing connections with other people in your world.

EXERCISE
Put Together a Winner's Circle

1. *Identify your support group.* Think about who's in your life—
the friends, family, colleagues, and loved ones you keep close.
Write a list of everyone you believe will be there for you to
cheer on your victories and support you in your triumphs.

2. *Evaluate your list.* Look over what you've written and ask
yourself if there are people close to you who are not on the list.
Are there loved ones—friends, family, colleagues, acquain-
tances—who you feel are there for you in bad times but not in
good ones? List them on a separate page.

3. *Rate your connections.* Looking quickly over your two lists, rate
everyone on a scale of 1 to 5:

> 1 = rarely have contact; contact at unpredictable times
> 2 = count on seeing or speaking to them, but rarely
>   (e.g., only on holidays or on yearly visits)
> 3 = see them fairly often but go through periods of losing
>   contact
> 4 = see or speak to them at least once a week
> 5 = see or speak to them several times a week

Use a different color for each rating.

4. *Evaluate your ratings.* Help yourself see your relationship patterns more clearly by reorganizing your lists. On five different
pages, write your 1s, 2s, 3s, 4s, and 5s. Then circle or highlight
in a bright color everyone on each list who is there for you in
times of joy and who would support you if you become more
successful. What have you discovered? Do you surround
yourself with people who are happy to support you in bad
times but not so willing to share your joys? Or have you put

together a true "winner's circle" of people who will support your progress and cheer for your triumphs?

5. *Consider your options.* Write at least one page to answer the following question: what can I do to create more support for my joys, my growth, and my success, however I define it?

6. *Check in with yourself.* Write for at least five minutes about your emotional, physical, and mental responses to this exercise. How do you feel? What have you learned? What would you like to do next?

Overcoming Isolation

- *Take a class.* Learning something new in the company of other people who care about the same topic is a terrific way to break through the isolation of a lonely, difficult time. Your class could be in a classroom—involving crafts, books, history, the arts— or it could involve more physical activity—kayaking, African dance, yoga, martial arts.

- *Join a group.* You may or may not find intimate friends and support in a group. But what you will surely find is a sense of being part of something larger than yourself, something that reminds you of your true, deep connection to the rest of the human race. A political action group, a religious group, a volunteer organization, even a book club gives you an anchor that can help you feel less isolated and more connected.

- *Volunteer.* If you're not willing to make a formal commitment to a group, start by volunteering. You can stuff envelopes for a political candidate, visit shut-ins, serve meals at a soup kitchen, pick up trash in a local park—anything that you do with others or for others, in a context that involves you with other people. You may or may not find intimacy. But you will find community and connection, and those can go a long way toward overcoming isolation.

- *Stay close to the friends you have.* If you're feeling lonely and isolated in your current circumstances, reach out to the people you know and love, even if they're in another city. Set up a regular phone date with a loved one. Agree to a weekly exchange of e-mails. Arrange with a friend to have Instant Messaging privileges when either of you is feeling blue. Even little reminders that someone out there loves and understands you can go a long way toward overcoming a lonely time.

- *Reach out to strangers.* Even if people you don't know can't offer intimacy, they are often eager to offer connection. Start a conversation with the waitress who brings you coffee or the clerk who takes your dry cleaning. Smile at the person sitting beside you on the bus or waiting in line with you at the post office. Be open to a casual chat or a friendly encounter that can make you feel seen, heard, and appreciated, even if it never goes any farther. Seeing the world as full of people you can connect to is a first step in overcoming your fear of isolation.

Sometimes we sabotage our progress because we're afraid that success—in love, work, or personal life—may leave us lonely. Sometimes, though, the issue is fear of not being a real man or a real woman, which we'll explore in the next chapter.

CHAPTER 8

Understand Your Fear
of Not Being a Real Man
or a Real Woman

M y patient Rosa was frustrated. A successful surgeon in her
midthirties, Rosa was an attractive, outgoing woman with a
sardonic sense of humor. She had come to me out of concern that
she hadn't yet found the stable, committed relationship she'd always wanted, the one that would allow her to combine her career
with the family she hoped to start. Although Rosa's job brought
her into contact with lots of unmarried men, she hadn't been seriously involved with anyone since she'd started med school.

"First, I need to lose twenty pounds," she'd tell me. "But with
the schedule I keep, who has time to exercise? I live on junk food
out of the vending machines, and I never get enough sleep. What
man is going to look at me? Plus, look at my schedule—the twelve-
hour shifts, the nights on call. No man is going to put up with
that."

I suggested to Rosa that since many of the men she met were

already working in the medical field, they might understand the demands of her job. If they were doctors themselves, they might even have similar schedules.

"Yeah, but that's my point," Rosa replied, exasperated that I was missing something that to her seemed so obvious. "They live like that. They don't want a wife who lives like that, too. They want someone who's going to be there when they get home from the hospital, not someone who's there all the time herself."

Rosa was especially vehement if she'd happened to catch an episode of the popular TV series *Grey's Anatomy*, which featured a predominantly female group of surgical interns as well as several top female surgeons.

"As if!" Rosa would say scornfully. "Sure you come in with a lot of other women—but the higher you climb, the fewer there are. And the ones at the top don't look like those actresses on TV, either, with their perfect hair and their gorgeous figures. They're sleep-deprived and haggard, like me. And the men on that show—supportive, admiring, happy to help a woman get to the next level—please! Don't make me laugh!"

As a professor at the Mount Sinai School of Medicine who's worked for years in hospitals and among doctors, I listened to Rosa with mixed feelings. Certainly there was a great deal of truth in what she said; in fact, I couldn't disagree with any of her specific points. Although conditions for women have improved immeasurably in the past thirty years, in medicine as in most professional fields, women still face prejudice, the glass ceiling, and innumerable difficulties combining family with career. While a male doctor can choose to marry a less career-oriented spouse who's willing to take on the bulk of the child-rearing and household responsibilities, that option is far less available to female physicians.

But I also felt that Rosa's own feelings about not being enough of a "real woman" were the hidden fears that she was refusing to look at. If I pointed out that she was the one identifying her weight and appearance as concerns and asked why she didn't take steps to correct the problems she herself had named, she'd insist that her schedule didn't leave her enough time, and besides, "Why should I have to care about things like that?" But if I pointed out that women of all shapes and sizes found happy marriages and asked why she couldn't accept her appearance exactly as it was and still feel sexual, womanly, and attractive, she'd insist that wasn't an option either. "Men want a certain package," she'd tell me, "and if a woman wants to get a man, she's got to provide it."

Rosa would neither accept nor reject society's idea of being a real woman, so she was stuck, unable to create her own vision of who she wanted to be. Fearing that she wasn't woman enough but unwilling to look closely at that fear, Rosa was keeping herself from taking any positive action, unconsciously sabotaging her own chances for the romantic happiness she sought.

My patient Paul had a parallel problem. Just as Rosa struggled with fears about not being a real woman, Paul, whom we met in the introduction, struggled with fears about not being a real man. When Paul decided not to go for partner in his law firm but instead to focus on his dream of being a serious amateur musician, he worried about what that meant for his manliness. Paul came from a working-class Jewish family where the idea of being a man was very much wrapped up with being a good provider. Paul's grandfather had abandoned his family, so Paul's father was especially invested in the idea that a real man sacrifices to provide for his wife and children. Even though Paul wasn't married and didn't have children, his parents viewed with horror what they saw as a frivolous decision to put his own pleasure ahead of his manly responsibilities.

Since Paul also wanted to be married and raise a family, he was further worried about the way women he knew might view his decision. "The women I've dated all had careers themselves," he told me. "But you could see that they were looking for a man who worked at least as hard as they did. Most of them wanted families, and they wanted a guy who'd be making enough money for them to stay home with the kids for at least five years, maybe longer. Plus they had a certain idea of the life they wanted— private schools for the kids, two nice cars, a summer place. I'm not sure they'd be interested in a man who wasn't going to pull his weight."

Fears of not being man enough were part of what had kept Paul from pursuing his dreams. But because Paul didn't really want the life of a hard-driven lawyer, he had also sabotaged his chances of making partner. Afraid that he wasn't a real man but unwilling to look at that fear, Paul was neither pursuing what he saw as a real man's duties nor striving for his own dream. Neither he nor Rosa was ready to confront their hidden fears, so both of them were stuck.

Not Enough of a Woman

Clearly, both men and women struggle with the fear of not being what their gender is conventionally supposed to be. But in my professional experience, this issue is far more pressing for women. I would almost go so far as to say that I've never treated a woman who wasn't struggling with it, whatever other issues were also important to her.

My female patients include some of our nation's top athletes, executives, and performers. They've worked for years to get where they are. Often they tell me, with total conviction, that they are wholeheartedly devoted to being the best they can be.

Then, as our conversations continue, their mixed feelings begin to emerge. In Rosa's case, her conflicts kept her from pursuing romance. Other women I've treated find themselves struggling with mysterious blocks to their professional progress. As did the other patients we've met, they experienced these obstacles as beyond their control. But often they were also creating their own roadblocks out of an unwillingness to confront their fears.

Maggie, for example, was a pro golfer who had recently gone into a slump. Eventually she realized that she'd always been worried about how athletic success would undermine her female identity. "It takes a pretty secure guy to handle a top athlete," she told me. "I'm literally a champion. So what does that make him?"

Tina was an actress who came to me when she started having disabling headaches that her doctors couldn't find a reason for. As we worked together, she realized how lonely and frightening she found it to be unlike the other women she knew. "My friends are always telling me to slow down, take it easy—it's as though they're telling me to be more like them," she said tearfully. "But I'm not like them. Yes, I want to make it—I want to be a great actress and to have all the chances in the world to do great work. I know I'm supposed to care more about people—I know I'm supposed to want that great guy and those wonderful kids—but my work is what I really love. What kind of a woman does that make me?"

Cicely was a promising attorney who was struggling to make partner. She came to me because she, like Paul, felt that something was mysteriously interfering with her ability to focus. One day she simply exploded in frustration. "I see how the guys in my office operate," she said. "The job comes first, before anything else. They don't care if anybody likes them, if anybody thinks they're attractive, if anybody's feelings get hurt. I want to go for partner, I really do. But I can't do it their way—and I don't know how else to do it."

In my view, Maggie's slump, Tina's headaches, and Cicely's loss of focus were all results of ignoring the same hidden fear: that if they pursued what they really wanted, they'd somehow lose their ability to be real women. For Maggie, the issue was desirability. She thought that men would find it hard to be attracted to a top athlete. Tina was worried about her ambition. She felt that her love of acting and her intense desire to succeed made her less of a woman than her more traditional female friends. Cicely's concern was her personal style. She wanted to succeed, but in her own way, and she feared that going wholeheartedly for professional success would mean giving up her female identity as a warm, caring, and attractive person.

For all of these women, I saw two problems. On the one hand, they really were in a difficult situation. Although in theory, women today have all the same chances as men, few women I've treated believe that's true. Statistics back them up: women still earn less than men, receive fewer promotions, and are unlikely to rise as high professionally. Women are still less likely than men to find supportive spouses who will take on the bulk of the family and household responsibility, and men are also more likely to seek partners who are younger and less professionally advanced than they are.

Moreover, the myth of the "nice girl" is still with us. Even when women are successful, they're supposed to act as though they don't care much about achieving, that being a "nice person" means more to them than winning. For example, when the TV series *Commander in Chief* featured Geena Davis as the nation's first woman president, the program went to great pains to point out that the Davis character had never wanted the presidency. Instead, she was thrust into office by the death of the president, and even then, she almost withdrew in favor of the Speaker of the House. In real life, it's impossible to achieve even the vice presidency without superhuman levels of ambition; no one who runs for that office does not also dream of winning the top position. But the fictional character had to be a nice girl, protesting that she'd never meant to rise this high.

Moreover, studies show that women who "act like men"— assertive, outspoken, ambitious—often face more on-the-job harassment than more traditionally feminine women. Jennifer I. Berdahl's 2007 article "The Sexual Harassment of Uppity Women" revealed the results of Berdahl's research: women who expressed typically "male" traits—even if they also expressed typically "female" traits, such as warmth and sensitivity—were more likely to have been harassed at work. Furthermore, women working in typically male environments, such as a manufacturing plant, were more likely to be harassed than women in more female fields, such as a community service center. Berdahl concluded that sexual harassment was often less a display of desire than a kind of gender policing, a way of telling women that they didn't belong in a certain environment or weren't allowed to act in certain ways.

Those are the objective problems, the social factors that make it tough for women. But my patients also struggled with an internal problem: the fear that if they pursued the life they really wanted, they would somehow lose their ability to be a real woman. Rosa, Maggie, Tina, and Cicely all feared not being real women—and they were all afraid to confront that fear. Their hidden fears were at best leaving them frustrated, stuck, and in a great deal of pain.

Women and the Motive to Avoid Success

As I looked for ways to help my female patients, I was struck by what Freud, the founder of psychoanalysis, had said about this issue. Writing in a time when professional careers for women were virtually unknown and when women were generally not supposed to work outside the home (though many did), Freud saw women as focused only upon their romantic goals—finding the man of their dreams. In his view, erotic or romantic success was all women really cared about.

Men, by contrast, seemed to want both romantic and career success, and they saw the two as going together. In fact, as Freud saw it, men viewed romantic success as a by-product of career success, imagining a devoted woman who cheered them on to fame and fortune or a beautiful maiden whose heart they won through their worldly triumphs.

For Freud, the idea that a woman might also want career success was unimaginable. Now, of course, we assume that women can and perhaps even should want to succeed in the workplace. But I had seen how many of my female patients struggled with the conflicts between success at work and fulfillment in love. Even though I started practicing at a time when women were supposed to be able to have it all, many of them didn't—and agonized over why they couldn't.

So I was fascinated when I came upon the work of pioneering psychologist Matina Horner, who gave these ideas a new twist in 1968. That was the year Horner conducted her landmark analysis of the syndrome she called the "motive to avoid success."

Like Freud, Horner thought that some people avoided success because they associated it with dire consequences. Given the negative view of working women that was popular at the time, Horner wondered whether women associated success with a loss of femininity, so she devised a study to find out. Working at the University of Michigan, Horner administered a simple test to ninety females and eighty-eight males, mainly freshmen and sophomores. The students were asked to write a story in response to a given cue. For women it was, "After first term finals, Anne finds herself at the top of her medical school class." Young men got the same cue, but with the name John instead of Anne.

Horner was shocked by what she found. The young men generally wrote happy, positive stories, predicting a bright future for John that included marriage and a family. Indeed, John's professional success was often described as enhancing his personal success, because it allowed him to provide for his family. As far as John was concerned, Freud's description was still accurate: career success made love more likely.

Anne's future was not nearly so bright. The young women described her as unhappy and lonely, adding frequently that she was unmarried. When Anne did have a family, she either neglected them or used them to further her own ambitions. The women who portrayed Anne as finding love insisted that she give up her success; one story suggested that Anne deliberately lower her own grade while helping her boyfriend to raise his. Eventually Anne dropped out of med school and married her boyfriend, who continued to study as Anne raised their family.

In other words, Horner concluded, women were afraid that career success would bring them not reward, but punishment. They worried that no man would want to marry a successful female professional, that such a woman would be an object of ridicule and scorn. Worse, they worried that to become such a success, they would also have to become people they themselves didn't like: aggressive, bitter, selfish. How, Horner asked, could women ever strive wholeheartedly for success in the workplace if that was their view?

Psychologists continue to argue about Horner's methods, analysis, and conclusions. But study after study supports the idea that women feel anxious about career success. In 1984, for example, researcher Gilah Leder conducted an expanded version of Horner's study, asking men and women to write about each other as well as about themselves. Sixteen years after Horner's work, Leder found that both sexes were still writing far more negatively about successful women than about successful men—and even more so if they were writing about women achieving success in a typically male field, such as mathematics.

In some ways, today is even worse than 1968, because now we have the illusion that the problem has been solved. So when my patients come up against these conflicts about being real women, they tend to blame themselves, assuming that every other woman has somehow made things work. Or they assume that successful women really are the nice girls they pretend to be, and they worry that their own drive and ambition are unwomanly. Meanwhile, they struggle with their own ideas about men and women, which are sometimes traditional, sometimes more adventurous—and often conflicted.

Are you trying to figure out your own ideas about men, women, work, and love? Take the following quiz on gender attitudes to learn more about what you really think—and how your opinions might be affecting your well-being.

QUIZ

What Are Your Attitudes about Gender?

For every question, read the example first as though it concerns one gender, and then as though it concerns the other. See how and whether your responses change when you alter the gender. Your focus is not to come up with a right answer but rather to discover what your gut response is and what attitudes, feelings, and assumptions about men and women float to the surface.

1. Terry is a forty-five-year-old married nurse who works part-time to care for the couple's three children, ages five, four, and two. Both members of the couple feel strongly about parents being the primary child-care people for children under five, and they had their children with the understanding that Terry was committed to caring for them. However, Terry is finding work as a nurse increasingly frustrating. It's hard to be always taking orders from the doctors, and often Terry feels that others don't respect the job. Plus, the pay isn't great—another sign that the job isn't respected. Now Terry has the chance to enter a demanding hospital program that puts candidates in line for administrative positions. Terry is already at the uppermost age limit for this program and is unlikely to get similar opportunities in the future. What do you think is the right thing for the couple?

   a. Terry enters the program, and Terry's spouse works part-time to share child care.

    b. Terry enters the program, and the family cuts back on expenses to pay for child care.

    c. Terry passes on the program and continues to work part-time as agreed.

    d. Some other solution: _____.

2. Sandy has been married for about ten years. The couple has two children, aged seven and nine. Both partners now work full-time and share child-care and household responsibilities. Sandy has always struggled with weight, but when the couple married, Sandy was able to stick to a rigorous diet and exercise plan. Since then, Sandy has gained thirty pounds. Sandy protests that work, child care, housework, and stress make it extremely difficult to lose weight. Sandy still gets flirtatious glances at work, but the spouse is unwilling to have sex with Sandy in this condition, and Sandy worries that an affair may be in the works. What do you think is the right thing for the couple?

    a. Sandy should make it a priority to lose weight and become more attractive to the spouse.

    b. The spouse should focus on Sandy's contributions to the marriage and consider the weight issue the spouse's problem, not Sandy's—particularly since other people find Sandy attractive.

    c. The couple should enter counseling with the understanding that each is conflicted about the marriage.

    d. Some other solution: _____.

3. Alex is an ambitious, hard-driving professional who earns $200,000 a year. Alex gets a great deal of pleasure from a demanding job that requires many nights and weekends. Alex also keeps fit with a rigorous gym schedule and a regular tennis game. Some friends say that Alex is a workaholic. Others consider Alex a catch: attractive, successful, charming, and

(according to previous relationships) good in bed. Recently Alex has been frustrated in attempts to find a romantic partner. Either it's impossible to meet anyone, or all the prospects seem to be low-energy, dependent people who will clearly want more of Alex's time and emotional energy than Alex is willing to give. What do you think Alex should do?

    a. Find new places to look for hard-driving, ambitious mates who will share Alex's energy level.

    b. Cut back on work and the gym to make more time for relationships.

    c. Reconsider the qualities Alex is seeking in a mate.

    d. Some other solution: _____.

4. Brett is a quiet, shy, gentle person who has a hard time approaching new people and making friends but who is dearly loved by many people. Friends will say that Brett is someone you can really count on in a pinch, someone you can always talk to, someone whose smile and kind words always lift their spirits. Brett has a decent job and does all right at it, but work is not a major focus. What Brett really loves is hiking, and Brett's life is organized around long hiking and camping trips, sometimes alone, sometimes with a hiking club. Recently Brett has had trouble finding a romantic partner. Brett feels too shy to attract much romantic attention. Although Brett has a strong sexual side, most people don't realize it until the fourth or fifth date. Brett actually has attracted quite a bit of interest—but all from bossy, dominant people who are too intense for Brett. What do you think Brett should do?

    a. Make more effort to reach out to shy, quiet people who resemble Brett.

    b. Find a more sexual style that will be more attractive to a potential romantic partner.

    c. Be patient and trust that the right person will discover Brett's special qualities.

d. Some other solution: _____.

5. Sean is nearly thirty-five years old and wants very much to start a family. Sean has been dating in a very committed, determined fashion, looking for a partner who also wants to raise children. Before Sean wanted to start a family, there was no shortage of dates and relationships, but this new intention seems to make it harder. Either Sean's romantic partners aren't sure about wanting children, or they're not interested in moving as quickly as Sean is. Sean is worried that time is running out. What do you think Sean should do?

   a. Consider being a single parent.
   b. Accept that children may not be in Sean's future.
   c. Find more creative ways to hook up with other family-minded partners.
   d. Some other solution: _____.

What did you think? Did you discover attitudes you didn't realize you had? Did clarifying your feelings about men's and women's roles bring any new insight? Did you perhaps even discover some attitudes about gender roles and responsibilities that might be getting in your way, attitudes that don't fit with your own best sense of who you are and what you're looking for in work and love? To consolidate what you learned, complete the following sentences:

1. I think men and women should have similar roles and responsibilities when it comes to _____, because

_____

_____.

2. I think men and women should have different roles and responsibilities when it comes to _____ because

_____

_____ .

3. My attitudes may create difficulties for me because _____

_____ .

4. My attitudes may make things easier for me because _____

_____ .

5. Something I would like to change about my attitudes toward gender is _____ because _____

_____ .

If you like, think further about what you've learned by writing for at least five minutes about your experience of taking this quiz.

SCIENCE MATTERS

Is Equality Bad for Your Health?

A 2007 study conducted by the Swedish National Institute of Public Health suggests that men and women who are professionally equal are more likely to suffer illness or disability. The report, published in the journal *Social Science and Medicine*, concluded that there might be "an unfortunate trade-off between gender equality as we know it and public health."

As a staunch believer in gender equality, I admit that my heart sank as I read those words. But then I read further. What the report really said was that we're in a time of transition, in which the attempts to reach gender equality have indeed made things more difficult for women. But the solution is not to backtrack, but rather to continue until "men also significantly alter their behaviour."

True, the report admitted, both women and men might suffer negative effects from this "unfinished equality." Women were facing greater burdens as they tried to balance career with family, even as they strove to achieve higher levels of career success. And men, too, were stressed as they gave up many of their old privileges.

But in the words of Anastasia de Waal, head of family policy at the British research institute Civitas, "what Sweden needs is complete gender equality with, for example, men entering the private sphere to the extent that women have entered the public." Rather than going back to a time of more defined roles and accepted inequality, the solution might be to go forward until equality is so acceptable that it no longer seems stressful.

Women at Odds

Although Rosa, Maggie, and Cicely were worried about the responses of men, my patient Tina was more concerned about relationships with her female friends. Likewise, many of the studies conducted by Heilman and her colleagues included female as well as male participants, all of whom seemed equally likely to rate successful women as unlikable. Indeed, a growing body of research suggests that women fear not only the negative responses of men but also the hostile response of other women, and that at issue is not only career success but also love, family, and any kind of personal happiness.

Much of this research is summed up in a recent book called *Tripping the Prom Queen: The Truth about Women and Rivalry* by gender expert Susan Shapiro Barash. Barash suggests that fear of female envy causes women to hold themselves back from success in a wide variety of spheres, including relationships, marriage, motherhood, and friendship, as well as in career matters and financial success. Even if women don't actually refrain from seeking promotions or pursuing romance, Barash argues, their anxiety about female rivalry poisons much of the pleasure they might otherwise get from their triumphs. Despite feminism's promise of sisterhood and solidarity, women are often afraid—rightly or wrongly—that their mothers, sisters, best friends, or colleagues will resent them for becoming happy, fulfilled, or successful in any domain: work, love, or personal life.

For example, Michael E. Hyland and Anthony V. Mancini found that women feared success because it might lead to loss of friendship. Likewise, Joseph Balkin discovered that female college students from working-class backgrounds were more likely to fear success when they had no friends who also were going to college. And my own work with patients such as Miriam, whose mother envied her romantic success, supports the idea that women's fears of other women's responses are frequently huge—if hidden— forces in their own lives.

So even when women get the love and marriage they say they want, they may continue to feel attacked by other women, even as they face new problems in dealing with their men. A 2006 study titled "What's Love Got to Do with It?" suggests that although women once hoped that more equality in marriage might make them happier, men are more likely to do the "emotion work" that satisfies women—talking about their own feelings, asking about their partner, spending time together, and so on—in relationships that are less egalitarian.

W. Bradford Wilcox and Steven L. Nock, sociologists at the University of Virginia, suggest that in relationships where men feel more secure and more powerful, they are more likely to be attentive to their partners, with the result that their wives are happier. Wilcox and Nock also suggest that women who feel more equal—and who have incomes and professional standing comparable to their husbands'—may feel freer to provoke conflicts, which drive the men away.

So once again, a woman who has achieved professional success may feel that she's hurt her chances of creating a happy marriage. If Wilcox and Nock are to be believed, the more successful a woman is in her career, the less likely she is to be happy in love. More happy, they believe, are women who hold traditional views of marriage, in which marriage itself is viewed as a positive good; such women are also likely to receive more institutional support from organized religion and other community groups. More happy as well are women whose marriages are divided according to traditional roles, in which the men know what's expected of them and feel good about providing it; that seems to free the men to do more of the "emotion work" that pleases the women.

As in the Swedish study, Wilcox and Nock's report indicates that being halfway between tradition and liberation is an uncomfortable place to be. As women and men rewrite their roles and relationships, conflicts increase; when everyone knows what's expected, conflict declines. However, once the genie is out of the bottle—once a woman has a taste for fulfilling her dreams of achieving something beyond the four walls of her home—it seems to me that the only way is forward. Going back to an earlier, simpler time with fewer choices is simply not an option.

Moving Forward

Where does all this leave Rosa, Maggie, Tina, and Cicely, and where does it leave you? We can take some comfort in a study by Liana C. Sayer and Suzanne M. Bianchi, University of Maryland researchers who reviewed the relationship between women's economic independence and the probability of divorce. Sayer and Bianchi found that although women's economic independence does allow women to divorce if they choose, a woman's job and bank account really don't predict the likelihood of divorce nearly as well as marital commitment and satisfaction. A woman who's earning her own living is free to leave a bad marriage—but she isn't any more likely to leave a good one.

We can also take comfort in the fact that on an individual level at least, new possibilities open up as soon as we become aware of the hidden fears and buried dreams we haven't been able to face. Only by looking clearly and compassionately at ourselves and our situation can we decide what we have control over, what we don't, and what we'd like to do about it.

Rosa, for example, needed to face her own complicated responses to her body and her traditionally male profession. As we worked together, Rosa came to realize that she'd never been quite sure of how to express her own sexual nature. If she presented herself as attractive, sexual, and open to a relationship, she felt—with some justification—that she wouldn't be taken as seriously in her profession. But if she presented herself as unattractive and uninterested in men, she felt hurt by the responses she got and anxious about her own sense of herself as a woman.

The key for Rosa was threefold. First, she had to decide what her own ideal sense of her body and her sexuality would be. What weight and appearance did she prefer? How much time and attention did she want to give her physical self in the form of careful eating, exercise, pampering, clothes shopping, and all the other work that goes into maintaining a female appearance? What style did she choose for work, for relaxing at home, for dating, for spending time with her friends? Learning to see herself through her own eyes rather than through other people's eyes wasn't easy for Rosa. In a culture that so trains women to see themselves from the outside, I don't think it's easy for any woman. But making that shift was crucial for Rosa, as for many of my patients. Otherwise, she'd always be stuck in a holding pattern: resenting the world's standards but refusing to stand up for her own.

Second, she had to decide what kinds of relationships she really wanted. Who was her ideal man, and what compromises was she willing to make? Again, this wasn't easy, because Rosa had long felt, with some justification, that most men didn't meet her standards. This created another kind of holding pattern: feeling frustrated with most of the guys she met but not really trusting her own judgments and responses. So Rosa would meet a guy, decide he was shallow, try to date him anyway, and then be frustrated that he hadn't responded to her. If she'd had the courage of her convictions—the courage of her true desires—she might have been more honest with herself, choosier, and perhaps less frustrated.

Third, Rosa had to demand more rigor from herself about what was really going on. Instead of a generalized frustration with "how bad it is," she had to get more specific about exactly what she could and couldn't change in any given situation. Then she had to commit to stop blaming herself for the things that weren't her fault and to focus on the part of the situation—however large or small—that she could change.

In a sense, Rosa had been taking both too much responsibility and not enough. On the one hand, instead of looking clearly at the genuine difficulties involved in being a female surgeon in a biased world, she wanted to blame herself for not being more thin, attractive, and charming. On the other hand, instead of being honest about how few men she felt met her standards, she wanted to be mad at them for not appreciating her.

Looking clearly at a difficult situation—she did face bias, both at work and in love—was sometimes painful for Rosa. But it also freed her from futile efforts and even more painful self-doubts. "I don't like what I see sometimes," she told me recently. "But I've learned that it's always better to see what's out there and then to do what I can about it." In fact, this new clarity seems to have freed Rosa to be more present in the world, so that her body, her sexuality, and her desire to connect are more visible and accessible to the men she meets. As a result, she's started to date again, and feels more hopeful about what the future might bring.

Maggie underwent a similar process of becoming clear with herself. She realized that her championship status might indeed make it more difficult for her to find a guy—but that any guy who couldn't handle a champion probably wouldn't interest her anyway. Knowing that she's the one who's being choosy rather than seeing herself as continually rejected has freed her as well, and she's managed to come out of her slump.

Tina, the actress, is still struggling with her sense of herself. It's hard for her to accept how different she is from the women she knows, and hard for her to imagine what her future might be if she doesn't enter the traditional marriage that she knows she doesn't want. But bringing her fears and dreams to the surface has at least freed her from the debilitating headaches. Whatever choices Tina makes, she's allowing herself to enjoy the journey while she makes them.

Cicely, like Paul, decided that some changes were in order. She left the high-pressured law firm where she'd been working because she realized it would be almost impossible for her to succeed there unless she adopted a completely different personal style. Working at a smaller, less prestigious firm is frustrating for her in some ways. She knows that if she makes partner here, she'll be earning significantly less money and won't have the kind of presence in the legal community that she'd once hoped for. She's not happy that she had to make the trade-off. But she feels that she read the situation correctly and made the best possible choice that the world offered her at the time. As a result, she has the satisfaction of feeling that she's doing her best work and enjoying it, even if there are some things she wishes she could change.

What about you? Do you see some ways to look more clearly at these issues and move forward in your life? Perhaps the following exercise will inspire you to new insight.

EXERCISE
*Visualizing Your Ideal Version
of Your Gender*

1. *Relax.* Visualize descending a flight of eighteen stairs, breathing and counting down so as to relax your body, clear your mind, and open your heart.

2. *Visualize yourself walking along a road.* Allow yourself to envision a pleasant journey along a road. It might be a trail through the woods, a highway through the country, a path that runs through towns and villages, or any other road that comes to mind. As always, use specific sensory details—from sight, hearing, smell, taste, and sensation—to allow the scene to become clearer, sharper, and more present.

3. *Choose your appearance.* Imagine that your first stop along this road is a place where helpers will assist you in looking exactly the way you feel best expresses your sexuality and your own version of being a man or a woman. Allow yourself to picture what this place might be, then see yourself entering it. See the people, creatures, or forces that are helping you, and feel yourself dropping any aspect of your appearance that does not fit the identity you know is truly yours. Imagine what you'd need to make your sense of yourself fit the way you appear. See your helpers providing you with whatever you need to express your true self. Are you presenting yourself more sexually? More professionally? With more strength? With more openness? How does your posture change? How does your facial expression alter? How do you feel inside? Experience these changes from the inside out as you continue to make specific choices for your hair, face, clothing, shoes, accessories, posture, and expression.

4. *View your appearance.* Envision your helpers providing you with a mirror that reflects back this ideal vision of your sexuality and your own ideal version of being a man or a woman. If you have more than one ideal version of yourself—perhaps one for work and one for romance—see each version appear in the mirror as you observe and take note.

5. *Integrate your appearance.* If you've seen yourself in different versions, think about how you might integrate aspects of these different versions to a single, unified person who reveals his or her sexual, professional, and personal natures all at once. Choose the clothes, hairstyle, accessories, posture, and facial expression that most express the person you know you really are.

6. *Continue on your journey.* Leave this first stop and continue walking along the road. Perhaps it's the same road as you imagined before; perhaps it has changed. Notice what it feels like to walk through the world with your true self on display. If you encounter anyone along the journey, notice what responses you get. Walk for a few minutes until you reach your second stop.

7. *Enter a workplace.* Take this new version of yourself into a place where you work. You might imagine a real-life work environment, present or past, or you might invent a place where you would like to work. Choose the place where you are most eager to display your new self. Enter this environment, notice whom you meet and what responses you get, and begin to do the work you most enjoy. Continue to notice sensory details—sight, hearing, smell, taste, and touch—to ground your experience of working as your new, visible self.

8. *Enter a romantic setting.* When you're ready to leave the workplace, continue along whichever road you choose until you're ready to enter a romantic setting. Again, it can be a real place where you've actually been, or a place of your imagination.

Envision a meeting with the person you'd most like to connect with romantically—either a real person or someone you're imagining. Notice every detail you can about this person—what you find attractive, what response you get—as well as observing how you behave. See yourself fulfill your best vision of what you could be as a romantic partner.

9. *Conclude the journey.* When you're ready, find a way to end the scene and allow yourself to return to your actual setting by climbing your flight of stairs as you breathe and count. Remain with your eyes closed, breathing deeply, as you review what you've experienced.

10. *Write about what you've learned.* Take at least ten minutes to record what you experienced. Then complete the following sentences:

   a. My ideal presentation of my sexuality and my ideal version of being a man or a woman would be _____
   _____.

   b. What I currently do that fits this ideal is _____
   _____.

   c. What I'd like to change to better fit this ideal would be
   _____.

   d. What I most liked about the way I was in the visualization was _____
   _____.

   e. One thing I could do tomorrow to re-create that part of myself would be _____
   _____.

Facing your fears about being a real woman or a real man can be tremendously liberating, freeing you to create the life you really want. Before you go on to that final step, however, there's one more fear we have to consider: fear of being trapped in a false dream.

CHAPTER 9

Uncover Your Fear of Being Trapped in a False Dream

L ia was a talented young woman poised on the brink of success as a budding pop star. After three years of touring, she'd finally attracted the attention of a major record label, which signed her to a multiyear contract.

Then Lia's troubles began. First, she had a serious falling out with her manager, a man who had been with her from the beginning of her career. Then, at an important business lunch, she had one drink too many and began insulting one of the executives, who was clearly put out by her behavior. Although she'd always been warm and courteous to the road crew, now she started finding fault with every detail of her concert dates—the dressing rooms, the sound equipment, the room-service menus at her hotel.

Within a few months of signing with the label, Lia seemed to have alienated virtually everyone associated with her career. In effect, she'd created her own private meltdown.

Finally, Lia came to me. As we talked through her experiences, I was struck by how contemptuously she spoke about the company that had signed her and the kind of music they usually produced. "They don't want a real voice out there," she said once. "They don't want a real woman singing, either. They just want a little plastic doll."

The more we talked, the clearer it became that Lia had serious doubts about the life of a major pop star. She loved to sing and to write music, but she didn't enjoy dressing in the sexy little outfits the company chose for her or taking part in the rock videos they produced, which she insisted were little better than soft-core porn. She was frustrated by the way fans insisted on hearing her familiar roster of hits and wouldn't even listen to the new music she wanted to explore. She had no doubts at all about music as a vocation, but she had serious questions about how to define her music career.

It wasn't easy for Lia to face her true feelings about the kind of success she really wanted. She'd wanted to believe that pursuing success would be a straight line for her, that her obvious talent, star quality, and good looks would send her right to the top of her profession. Now she had to recognize that she might not be able to have it all, that her version of musical success might involve less money, recognition, and security than a more conventional career, even if it also brought her more artistic and personal satisfaction.

Lia wasn't happy with these potential limits, but she was even less comfortable acknowledging how unusual her ideas were in the world of popular music. "Why can't I just be like everybody else?" she asked me once, only half joking. "Why do these things bother me when everybody else seems okay with them?"

Lia's journey toward self-definition had its difficult moments, but in the end, it was a journey of liberation that freed her from the meaningless fights and petty blowups she'd been provoking among her colleagues and associates. Because Lia genuinely wanted goals that were not shared by many people in her profession, she had to make more conscious choices than many of her fellow singers and be ready to accept the consequences of these choices. This wasn't an easy process but, Lia agreed, it was definitely preferable to a mysterious meltdown that alienated the people who had always supported her. The price of self-awareness was giving up some of her unrealistic hopes. But the benefits far outweighed the price.

The Seduction of a False Dream

Most of us may not be interested in the kind of stardom that Lia sought. But many of us struggle with some of the same issues that were so difficult for her. We live in a culture that's highly focused on particular visions of success, love, and personal happiness. We're all supposed to want financial security, a substantial income, and a prestigious job. We're also supposed to want true love, a secure marriage, and a happy family. We're supposed to be thin, attractive, and fit, and to attract partners who have the same qualities. We're supposed to go for what we want, express serenity about what we can't have, be high-achieving individuals, and yet somehow also fit in with the group, making others feel comfortable.

Not all of us want these things—yet many of us feel we should or believe we do. Like Lia, we may fear being—or feeling—*different*, unwilling to pursue our dreams because we don't want to threaten our family, our loved ones, our community. We may simply not like being the only one who has an unusual dream, or we may fear—often for good reason—that pursuing that dream will bring retaliation from loved ones, colleagues, employers, or members of our community. The artist who has an unusual perspective, the activist who has an alternative vision for society, the lover who desires a sexual relationship that's considered unconventional are striking examples of people with unusual dreams. But many of us also experience quieter, less dramatic versions of this conflict—and live in fear of the consequences.

Paul, for example, dreamed of a satisfying life as an amateur musician, a life in which career and financial security were far less important than personal satisfaction. Fear of being trapped in a false dream had led Paul to secretly sabotage his own efforts to make partner at his high-powered law firm. Yet Paul also feared facing his buried dream, unwilling to disappoint his family or alienate a potential spouse.

Likewise, my patient Ronnie feared being trapped in a false dream of domesticity. An attractive, forthright woman in her midthirties, Ronnie insisted that she wanted marriage and a family. She'd always loved kids, and she'd had several satisfying relationships with men. But when it came to creating a more committed, domestic life, Ronnie balked, without ever quite realizing that she was sabotaging her chances to get the life she claimed to want. She'd meet a great guy—and immediately find a million little things that were wrong with him. She'd meet a Don Juan—and quickly decide that she'd fallen in love. She'd avidly pursue a man who seemed only partially interested—and then, when he finally responded, she'd suddenly, mysteriously lose interest.

Nor could Ronnie express clearly what she wanted. "I want what everybody wants—marriage and a family," she'd say. But whenever I asked her to describe this marriage or to paint a picture of the relationship she sought, she spoke in vague terms and was clearly uncomfortable discussing the matter at all.

Gradually a different picture began to emerge. What Ronnie really wanted, she realized, was a more independent kind of partnership—a committed relationship with a man in which both parties lived apart and saw each other several nights a week. Although Ronnie did love children, she didn't really want the primary responsibility of caring for kids of her own; she preferred having the freedom to travel, to work late without guilt, to become absorbed in other aspects of her life.

Ronnie was extremely uncomfortable with this less conventional vision. She had a hard time accepting that what she really wanted was a childless life and a committed lover with whom she did not share a home. But even when she couldn't quite face what she really wanted, a deep part of her understood what she didn't want. As a result, she was sabotaging herself every step of the way—making relationship choices that were guaranteed to keep her out of a traditional marriage. Maybe she wasn't ready to pursue her real dream, but she was going to make sure, even if unconsciously, that she didn't get trapped in a false dream. As a result, she was stuck.

Eventually Ronnie came to see how she was sabotaging herself, but she was reluctant to own up to her nontraditional desires. "If I don't have children, won't I regret it?" she kept asking me.

"You may well regret not having children," I told her. "On the other hand, if you have children and you miss out on other things, won't you regret that, too?"

Ronnie looked at me doubtfully. "Everybody says that once you have children, nothing else matters," she said. "They say that once you hold your baby in your arms, you're willing to make any sacrifice."

"That's what 'everybody' says," I responded. "What do you say?"

Ronnie shook her head and changed the subject. "What kind of man is going to want the kind of relationship I'm describing? Either he'll be frustrated that I won't marry him, or he'll be a total hound, unwilling to make any kind of commitment at all. Aren't I just being unrealistic?"

"Suppose that what you want is more difficult to achieve than other types of relationships," I responded. "Would you prefer to settle for something you don't really want?"

"But I should want it, shouldn't I?" Ronnie burst out. "I should want children, I should want a good, committed relationship. Isn't that why I'm in therapy, so I can learn to want what's good for me?"

Although neither Ronnie nor Paul was gay, both of them reminded me of patients I'd treated who were, people who struggled with their own desires for a relationship or an entire life that many people considered illegitimate, immature, or simply "wrong." Although many people—gay and straight—are perfectly comfortable with unusual or unconventional desires, many of us have a deep longing to be like everybody else. When we realize that our dreams may take us further from our families, our loved ones, and our communities than we'd prefer, we may try to bury those dreams and choose a false dream instead. We go for versions of success, love, and personal happiness that seem to make us more like other people, instead of being true to our real dreams.

But then, because we don't really want those false dreams, we make sure we don't get them. Like Paul, we lose focus just as we're about to achieve a professional goal. Or like Ronnie, we can't seem to manage the kind of relationship we say we want. Like Lia, we may pick fights with friends, loved ones, colleagues, or employers, finding fault with trivial issues so we can avoid the real problem. Just as I did when I prevented myself from going to medical school, we make sure that we can't achieve our false dream—even if we don't realize that's what we're doing. Perhaps we are afraid of owning up to our real dreams—but we fear being trapped in a false dream as well.

Do You Fear Being Trapped
in a False Dream?

Is fear of a false dream one of the hidden fears that's secretly shaping your life? Use the following checklist to begin exploring the issue.

CHECKLIST

Is Fear of a False Dream Holding Me Back?

☐ I have clear, focused goals for myself in work, love, and/or my personal life, and I can't understand why I haven't made more progress toward them.

☐ My friends, family, and/or loved ones often express skepticism about what I say I want for myself.

☐ When I think about a goal I haven't reached, I can't list three specific actions I've taken to reach it over the past year.

☐ When I think about a goal I haven't reached, I feel at the end of my rope, unable to imagine what actions I could take.

☐ When I think about a goal I haven't reached, I feel exhausted and depressed.

☐ I know exactly what I need to do to reach my goal, but the very idea fills me with dread, despair, or exhaustion.

☐ When I start to define my goals, I find myself confused.

☐ When I start to define my goals, I find myself feeling bored.

☐ When I start to define my goals, I find myself feeling angry about the situation or about something that seems completely irrelevant.

☐ If I ask myself why I haven't achieved my goals so far, I either get bogged down in a welter of little details or I feel more vaguely that "it just didn't work out."

☐ I have a very clear idea of my goals, but when I think about those goals, I feel depressed, defeated, anxious, or angry.

☐ I believe if I achieved my goals, my family would be thrilled.

☐ I believe if I achieved my goals, my family would be upset.

☐   I believe if I achieved my goals, my loved ones and friends would be thrilled.

☐   I believe if I achieved my goals, my loved ones and friends would be upset.

Of course, there are many different interpretations for just about every item on this list. Sometimes it simply is hard to pursue our dreams; sometimes we do encounter a series of defeats that lays us low, or anticipate a set of obstacles that fills us with fear. Certainly we can be aware that our families, loved ones, and friends may have strong feelings about our dreams without necessarily letting them determine our goals. But if you feel confused about why you can't achieve what you say you want, consider the possibility that what you're seeking is a false dream, created to hide your deeper, truer desire for a more genuine dream. Consider, too, that you fear achieving the false dream at least as much as acknowledging the real one, which may be why you feel stuck.

If you think that fear of a false dream may be keeping you from getting the life you really want, you might want to go back to chapter 2 and reexamine the questionnaire "Am I Pursuing Goals That I Truly Desire?" on pages 43–48. You might also review your responses to the exercises "Visualize Your Life's Path" (on pages 49–51) and "Invite Your Passion to Fuel Your Journey" (on pages 52–54). You can use the following exercise to go deeper still.

EXERCISE
Waking from a False Dream

1. *Relax.* As always, start by seeing yourself descending a flight of stairs, counting backward from eighteen at the top to one at

the bottom and breathing deeply at each step. Keep your eyes closed.

2. *Select a goal that you feel may be a false dream.* You might choose a goal that involves work, love, or your personal life. Consider choosing a goal that has you baffled, one that seems mysteriously out of your grasp, leaving you confused and frustrated about your puzzling inability to make more progress.

3. *Visualize yourself walking in a pleasant landscape.* Allow your mind to create a beautiful, peaceful environment that fills you with pleasure. See yourself moving easily through these lovely surroundings, enjoying every step. For the moment, forget about your chosen goal completely. Focus only on the pleasure of your journey.

4. *Imagine that your path is taking you toward the goal you've chosen.* Notice how you feel when you introduce this element into the picture. Do you feel a quickening of desire, an increased energy, a heightened pleasure? Or do you feel a sudden dread, a rush of anxiety, anger, or confusion? Try not to judge any of your feelings. Simply allow yourself to experience them as you continue.

5. *Continue moving toward your chosen goal.* As you move toward your goal, notice what's happening to the landscape around you. Has it become more pleasant or less so? Is the road rougher, smoother, or different in some other way? Have the colors faded or grown more vivid? Does the light change? The weather? The landmarks? Again, try to observe without judging.

6. *As you continue, notice a detour.* See the path you're taking branch off into two choices. Notice your first impulse—is it to stay on your current path, or go somewhere new? Notice, too, how you felt when you became aware of the new path and realized that you had another choice. Finally, see whether

you have any idea where the new path leads. Does it feel mysterious, or are you pretty sure you know where it would take you? You might even look around for a signpost to see if you can find out more.

7. *Decide which path you prefer and continue on that one.* See yourself continuing on your old or your new path. Once again, notice how you feel. Notice, too, what the landscape is like, including the road itself, the surroundings, the weather, and any other elements of your experience.

8. *Prepare to encounter a helper.* See a sign indicating that you're about to meet someone whom you consider comforting, supportive, and wise. This may be a person in your past or present life; a person you have heard of, such as a religious figure or a celebrity; a person you imagine; or some other creature, such as an animal or a mythical being. Your helper is someone you trust completely to give you the best possible advice, without judgment or criticism; someone who approves completely of your best self and wants only what's best for you. Take a few moments to prepare yourself for this meeting. Visualize your helper and decide what question you'd like to ask about your path.

9. *Encounter your helper.* See yourself meeting the helper you've imagined. You might stop walking and join your helper in an environment of your choice, or you might continue down the road with your helper by your side. As always, notice both how you feel and what the landscape, weather, and road are like.

10. *Ask your helper about your path and listen to the answer.* Allow the conversation to continue as long as you like. Ask whatever questions are on your mind and pay attention to the responses you get.

11. *Decide what you'd like to do next.* Now that your helper has spoken with you, choose what you'd like to do next:

continue on your path, choose a new path, rest for a while, or take some other action. Stay with your decision for a few moments, noticing both how you feel and the environment you've visualized.

12. *When you're ready, return to the present.* Remind yourself that you can always return to your chosen path and your chosen helper. Then allow the visualization to dissolve as you remount the stairs, breathing and counting up at each step.

13. *Record the experience.* Check in with your body and your feelings. Then write for at least five minutes about what happened, noting any discoveries you've made about your false dreams and your true dreams. If you find it helpful, structure your writing around the following questions:
    - What false dream have I been pursuing?
    - Why have I clung to my false dream?
    - What price have I paid for my false dream?
    - What benefit have I gotten from it?
    - What would it take to let go of my false dream and pursue a true one?
    - What might that cost me? How might I benefit?
    - What true dream might I pursue instead of the false one?

The Myth of Having It All

As Ronnie and I continued to talk about what she wanted, she kept returning to the same two questions: "Won't I regret not having children?" and "Is it realistic to try to get the kind of relationship I want?" As I watched her struggle with these complex issues,

I was struck by the assumptions that seemed to lie underneath. It seemed to me that Ronnie, like many of us, had come to believe there was a way to "have it all," as though a healthy person could expect to achieve a life without regret. Instead of accepting that every major life choice brings with it roads not taken, Ronnie seemed to think that it was in her power to make such good choices that she'd never miss what she didn't have.

Certainly Ronnie might always feel a certain loss in not having had children. But it was also possible that if she did have children, she'd feel some loss and regret over what she had missed in that case. Both desires—to have children and not to have them— might be equally genuine, equally heartfelt, but clearly, Ronnie couldn't have both. Eventually she would have to choose (or life would choose for her). Whichever choice she made, she would inevitably feel some regret—not because she'd chosen wrong but because life simply doesn't allow us to have everything we can imagine.

Likewise, when Ronnie thought about wanting a somewhat unconventional relationship, she spoke about how "unrealistic" it was, as though wanting a conventional relationship were a safe or an easy choice. True, by wanting a more unusual arrangement, Ronnie might be limiting her choice of partners, since most men who want a committed relationship probably want a more traditional kind of marriage. Ronnie may have been right to believe that a man who sought a more unusual commitment might be harder to find than an ordinary marriage-minded man.

On the other hand, I'd certainly known plenty of people, inside and outside my practice, who had trouble finding happiness in more conventional versions of marriage. People with more conventional visions of relationship also have trouble finding marriage partners, and people who entered traditional marriages also face unhappy periods in their relationships. No relationship guarantees happiness, and no good or lasting relationship is necessarily easy to find or maintain.

In any case, since Ronnie was so actively—if unconsciously—refusing to enter a more conventional relationship, the point seemed almost moot. Instead of trying to make herself want a relationship that she didn't want just because it might be easier to get, I thought she'd do better to connect more deeply to her passion for the kind of relationship she did want. At least that way, she'd be wholeheartedly pursuing the life she wanted, which would vastly increase her chances of getting it.

If you, too, feel you may be drawn to an unconventional dream, I would advise you to define it and pursue it rather than trying to convince yourself to want something simpler or more conventional. I'm not advising you to ask for the moon or to pursue an impossible goal. I am suggesting that you consider whether your fear of being trapped in a false dream is keeping you stuck and then do the hard but necessary work of connecting to your true dream. It may be hard to achieve, and it may involve a certain amount of regret, loss, and compromise—but what doesn't? At least you'll know you're trying for what you really want, instead of sabotaging your efforts to get something you don't really want.

Ronnie struggled with these issues for a long time, but finally she came to terms with them. She began to see that even if she thought she'd be happier wanting a traditional marriage and children, she couldn't get herself to do more than pay lip service to that false dream. Meanwhile, she was wasting valuable time and energy making herself miserable over not getting something she didn't really want.

"It's like that old joke," she told me one day, "you know, the one where someone asks a man how he likes the food at his hotel? 'Oh,' he says, 'the food is terrible—and such small portions!' If I'm going to try to get bigger portions of something, I guess it should be something truly delicious."

In part one, you identified your buried dreams. In part two, you explored your hidden fears. Now it's time for part three, "Decide What Matters Most."

PART THREE

Decide What Matters Most

CHAPTER 10

Get in Touch with Reality

Lacey had been playing golf since she was five years old, and she'd been groomed to become a champion pretty much that entire time. Her mother had always loved sports but had grown up at a time when very few women strove for the highest ranks of athletic success, and she'd recognized in Lacey a chance to relive her own struggles as a female athlete. Lacey's father was a hard-driving lawyer who also loved golf and who appreciated his daughter's ambition. When Lacey first came to see me, she presented her family as the reason for her success and described herself as lucky to have such supportive parents.

Yet Lacey had begun to choke at key moments of important matches—flubs she found all the more upsetting because until recently she'd been known for her calm demeanor and her focused way of handling competition. She'd also begun to lose her temper—little blowups with her caddie, her swing coach, and her opponents—which she also found disturbing. "I love golf," she insisted, clearly fighting back the tears. "I'm so lucky to be able to play at this level. I've worked so hard to get here. And now I'm acting so badly—and I don't even recognize myself."

It seemed clear to me that Lacey was wrestling with a number of different fears she'd never fully come to terms with. And indeed, as we talked, Lacey began to express ways in which she experienced her mother's envy. "I feel like I'm letting her down if I don't make it, and hurting her feelings if I do," she said once. "She's sacrificed so much to get me where I am; no one could have been more supportive. But I know she must also wonder what if it was her playing at this level."

I asked Lacey what she imagined her mother's reaction would be if Lacey quit the sport. Lacey looked horrified. "It would kill her," she said immediately.

Then I asked Lacey how her mother would feel if Lacey became the champion she hoped to be. Lacey shook her head. "Maybe that would kill her, too," she said slowly.

At the same time, Lacey was frustrated with her father, who seemed to appreciate her ambition but didn't seem able to handle the times when she felt weak or despairing. During this period of choking, Lacey told me, he seemed almost frightened. "I feel like I'm keeping them both going," she said at the end of one session. "Like if I couldn't maintain this level, what would happen to them?"

In addition to the issues with her parents, Lacey felt a number of conflicts about how she could maintain her sense of being a desirable woman. When I asked her what the perfect woman should look like, she became almost angry. "Well, she wouldn't be fat," Lacey burst out, "but she wouldn't be hard and muscular, either." Lacey told me that she loved how she looked in her golf outfits but never quite felt like she'd chosen the right clothes the rest of the time. "I'm either too sporty or trying too hard," she said once. "Like I'm either an athlete or soooo girly, but I don't think either of those looks is really me."

Clearly, Lacey was struggling with a number of obstacles as she tried to get the life she wanted. She was contending with fear of her mother's envy, fear of her own anger toward both her parents, fear of losing not being a real woman. But it also was clear that she loved golf and that becoming a champion was a genuine dream, one she'd been seeking her whole life.

Through the work we did together, Lacey became aware of her fears as well as her dreams. But she faced one final step: putting her fears into perspective. To get the life she really wanted, Lacey had to ask herself two questions:

1. How likely is it that my fears will come to pass?

2. How bad will it be if they do?

A Reality-Based Approach

As I work with my patients, I'm struck by how many of them see therapy as a place to focus on their feelings. While this is clearly a hugely important aspect of doing therapy, I think it's only a first step. The ultimate goal of therapy or any other process of self-discovery, it seems to me, is to see reality in a clear and reliable way. If you don't have a realistic picture of what your options and obstacles are, how can you make good choices? Sometimes you may need to connect with your childhood feelings and perceptions so you can understand how they color your present worldview. But eventually you need to see things as they are now and to make choices based on your current, adult self.

Recall, for example, that my patient Paul feared financial insecurity, a fear that made it difficult for him to walk away from his chance to become a partner at his prestigious law firm. Paul's first step was to acknowledge his fear. But simply knowing that he was frightened didn't tell him everything he needed to know. He also had to develop a realistic picture of just how great his financial risk might have been and to decide how great a risk he was willing to take.

So after Paul realized that his fears were leading him to sabotage himself, he began to ask himself tough questions about those fears. What kind of financial insecurity was he actually risking? Was he facing homelessness, a significant drop in income, or only a minor inconvenience while he looked for other work? Was his financial future simply unknowable, with no way to determine whether he was risking destitution or simply a few overdue bills? Or were there some boundaries to his risk, ways of figuring out the worst it can get and what was most likely? Until Paul could look realistically at those issues, he couldn't know whether his fears were justified, and he couldn't make good choices about his next step.

Likewise, you'll recall that Paul feared his parents' disapproval. So he also had to ask himself whether his parents would, in fact, disapprove of his choice. Had he been exaggerating their potential response? Perhaps his parents had worried about his future when he was younger, but now they trusted him to take care of himself. Or maybe, now that they were older, they had become more preoccupied with their own lives and less invested in Paul's. Perhaps his parents would disapprove, but only mildly. Or perhaps the worst of Paul's fears were absolutely justified, and his parents would greet the news of him leaving the law firm with sorrow, rage, and insulting remarks about Paul's lack of responsibility, saying that his actions were killing his mother or were a slap in his father's face. It was important for Paul to look rationally at what he might expect and not simply to assume the worst.

Having explored what his parents' reactions might be, Paul then had to ask himself how much those reactions mattered to him. Suppose his parents did react as badly as he feared. Was avoiding that reaction worth staying in a situation that he disliked? Was their disapproval more important to Paul than his own satisfaction?

Perhaps it was, and perhaps getting in touch with that opinion would give Paul the boost he needed to overcome his lack of focus and become a partner. Or perhaps Paul's own pleasure meant more to him than pleasing his parents—a discovery that might help him find the energy to leave his law firm. Either way, Paul would have made a conscious choice that worked for him rather than being driven by fears and judgments he'd never really faced.

Likewise, Lacey had to ask herself some tough questions. She had to decide how realistic were her fears of her mother's envy, her anger at her parents, and not being a real woman. Were they issues she should take seriously? Or were they simply left over from childhood fears, issues that would dissolve as soon as she looked at them closely?

If Lacey did decide that some or all of her fears were justified, she would then have to decide how much space she wanted to give them. How important were her parents' reactions to her? How much did it matter to her to be a real woman? What kind of time, energy, risk, and commitment did she want to invest in solving the problems she had identified?

Although I firmly believe it's good to ask these questions, I have a lot of sympathy with how hard it is to come up with good answers. Our fears, hopes, and biases often keep us from seeing things clearly, and our unreliable memories make it even harder. Science has a lot to tell us about how our faulty memories can make it harder to predict the future. So let's take a closer look at the science of memory.

Memory and Emotion

It's well known among cognitive psychologists that we are far more likely to remember unusual events than ordinary ones. Generally, we're going to remember that one time Dad hit the ceiling or that single instance when Mom broke down in tears at a family dinner, rather than the thousands of relatively peaceful family meals. Likewise, if Dad was usually quiet and restrained, we're likely to remember the time he beamed at us with pride, while if Mom was usually more fearful, the time she said "I trust you completely" is what's going to stick in our mind. Whether our atypical memories are good or bad, we tend to remember them more readily than the run-of-the-mill events that happened every day.

By itself, this trick of memory probably wouldn't matter very much. After all, unusual events give life its color, drama, and texture. We should remember them, and we do.

The problem comes when we base our expectations of the future on these unusual memories. We recall the worst fight we ever had with our folks and then live in fear of it for the rest of our lives. Or we recall the best time we ever shared as a family and then feel perpetually disappointed that other family events don't meet that standard. Our memory's focus on the unusual can distort our ability to predict the future.

This was a topic that interested Harvard psychologists Carey K. Morewedge and Daniel T. Gilbert, along with their University of Virginia colleague Timothy D. Wilson. Together they studied the relationship between unusual memories and distorted predictions, and then published their findings in an article called "The Least Likely of Times: How Remembering the Past Biases Forecasts of the Future."

The team began by considering other studies that had explored what scientists refer to as impact bias—our memory's bias toward events that had unusual impact. These studies suggest that people expect to feel more intensely worse after negative events and better after positive ones than they usually end up feeling, and that this is especially true if the negative and the positive events they're trying to predict are similar to experiences they've had in the past. That fabulous or horrible family dinner is what sticks in our mind, biasing our expectations of all other family dinners. It's the unusual events that come most readily to mind, but we don't necessarily think of them as unusual.

The researchers wondered what would happen if they helped people put their memories into perspective. In their first study, they approached people on a subway platform and asked them different types of questions. One group was asked to describe an instance in which they missed their train (free recallers). Another was asked to describe the worst instance of missing a train (biased recallers). The third was asked to describe three instances of missing a train (varied recallers). Participants were then asked to rate how they'd felt about missing the train, and finally, invited to predict how they'd felt if they missed their train that day.

As the researchers expected, the free and biased recallers were most likely to come up with negative experiences of missing a train, probably because these were the most intense and therefore the easiest to remember. By contrast, the varied recallers—encouraged to come up with several examples—were more likely to remember at least one positive experience resulting from a missed train.

Even more interesting was the way these different recallers used their memories to anticipate the future. The free recallers, who'd been left to their own devices, expected to feel very unhappy if they missed their train probably because they'd quickly recalled an unusually bad experience with a missed train. But the biased recallers, who knew they'd chosen the worst instance of missing a train, were able to put the memory in perspective and didn't expect to be as unhappy. Interestingly, they made the same moderate predictions as the varied recallers, who'd been invited to recall more varied experiences. Just a little perspective made the future look brighter.

The team conducted a second study, in which they asked a number of Harvard football fans to predict how they'd feel if their team won. Again, they asked free recallers to simply describe a winning game (expecting that these free recallers would automatically think of an unusually good winning game). Biased recallers were explicitly asked to describe the best winning game they could remember, while varied recallers were asked to describe three winning games.

Then researchers asked people to predict how they'd feel if Harvard won that day. Once again, the free recallers predicted the most intense responses, presumably because they were unconsciously expecting that today's anticipated victory would be as satisfying as the game they'd remembered. Since they'd quickly remembered the best game, they based their predictions on that and unknowingly set themselves up for disappointment. By contrast, the biased and varied recallers, who'd been helped to put their best memories into perspective, were again more measured in their predictions.

Finally, the team studied another group of sports fans, this time at a Boston Red Sox baseball game. In this third study, the free recallers were asked to describe a game that the Red Sox won, while the biased recallers were asked to describe their best memory of a Red Sox victory. A third group, the nonrecallers, were asked no questions at all about previous games. Then all three groups were asked to predict how much they'd enjoy the game that day. Finally, the free and biased recallers were asked to rate their enjoyment of the games they'd recalled.

Significantly, both the free and the biased recallers rated their good memories equally positively. It would seem that when given free rein to remember a game, people quickly remember the best game. But again, when asked to predict how they'd feel about the current game, the biased recallers made more moderate predictions, presumably because they knew that they'd remembered an unusually good game and didn't expect the current game to match that standard.

By contrast, both the free recallers and the nonrecallers made more extravagant predictions about the current game, presumably because both groups were basing their predictions on unusually good memories. Even though the nonrecallers hadn't been asked to recall a game, they seemed to draw quickly on their best, most vivid, and least representative memories to make predictions, just as the free recallers did.

The researchers concluded that unless we're specifically cued to put things in perspective, we're likely to make predictions based on memories that are biased toward the atypical, whether unusually good or especially bad. Knowing that, we can use it to our advantage. For example, the researchers suggest, if you're scared of going to the dentist, try to remember the worst time you ever had in the dentist's chair, describing it to yourself or to a loved one in all its painful detail. That's probably the memory you most associate with the dentist, but you may not be aware either that it's the worst or that you're making all your predictions based on that unusual experience. Once you do distinguish between the worst and the typical, you'll be able to make better predictions.

I think we can use that knowledge to help us face our fears in general. Those of us who fear failure, mediocrity, success, envy, isolation, guilt, anger, not being a real man or a real woman, or even fear itself, should realize that our fears are probably based on the most painful experiences we've ever had with those emotions. But these most painful experiences are not the most typical. Putting our memories in perspective can help us get a grip on our fears.

Remembering Emotion

It's not only that our emotions distort our memories. We also harbor incorrect memories of emotions themselves. How we feel about something now leads us to distort how we felt about it in the past and perhaps to predict wrongly how we might feel about it in the future. Accordingly, when psychologists Linda J. Levine and Martin A. Safer reviewed the literature about how accurately people recalled their own emotions, they turned up some surprising discoveries.

The authors began by speculating that we've developed the capacity to recall emotions in order to be able to respond quickly to highly charged situations. If our ancestors had a run-in with a saber-toothed tiger, for example, they didn't have to remember a lot of detail about the encounter. The next time they saw the beast, they could just remember their fear and run for the hills.

Perhaps because emotions are such an important guide to action, we do seem to recall our emotions fairly accurately. However, our current emotional state can affect our memories. For example, one group of widows and widowers were asked to rate the intensity of their grief six months after the death of their spouse. Then, five years after their loss, they were asked to rate their grief again, both in the present and at that six-month mark. A significant number tended to project their present feelings into the past. Now that their grief was less intense, they recalled their previous grief as being far less intense than they'd rated it at the time.

Another set of studies concerned students who were asked about their anxiety levels regarding an upcoming exam. They were then asked afterward how they'd felt before the test. Students who'd done well on the exam underestimated the anxiety they'd felt before, while students who found they'd done poorly overestimated how nervous they'd been. It seems that we're constantly revising the memories of how we felt, perhaps because we're more interested in choosing actions for the future than in being accurate about the past.

Sometimes our misremembering can distort the truth. One study, for example, tracked wives over twenty years of marriage. When wives were asked to recall how they'd felt ten years earlier, they often reported higher levels of dissatisfaction than they'd described at the time along with high levels of current satisfaction. In other words, the wives were constructing a story in which they'd moved from less satisfied to more satisfied. They were unconsciously falsifying their memories to make themselves feel better about where they were now.

Trauma victims have sometimes responded in similar ways. If they are still doing badly several weeks or months after the trauma, they look for some hope, and they find it in revising the past. If they recall having felt worse right after the trauma than they actually did, they can point to their current shaky condition as an improvement. They may not have improved very much, but they unconsciously falsify their memories to feel that they did.

Likewise, a study of patients who were leaving therapy showed that almost two-thirds overestimated how distressed they'd been when they first entered therapy. Significantly, the patients who'd improved the most tended to underestimate their previous distress. Now that they were feeling better, they couldn't quite recall how bad they'd once felt. But the patients who'd improved less had to find some grounds for feeling good about themselves. So they exaggerated how bad they'd once felt in order to show that since then, they had improved.

After evaluating these studies, Levine and Safer came to a conclusion that I think has tremendous significance for all of us. People who have coped successfully with a difficult experience, they write, tend to recall their past emotions as pretty much like their present ones. Once they have successfully met their challenges, they forget the anxiety, distress, and sorrow with which they once struggled.

By contrast, people who are still actively coping with an emotional experience tend to exaggerate their past distress. Seeking some kind of comfort, they insist, not very accurately, that they used to feel much worse than they do now.

Why is this important? Because while we are still struggling with the hidden fears I've described in part two, we tend to remember our past experiences with them as much worse than they were. Then, as we just learned, we tend to use these unusually bad memories to predict the future. Suddenly we're caught in a vicious cycle.

For example, suppose you've had a bad experience with a romance. Now you're in a new relationship, but you're still afraid of the rejection and pain you felt before. Your tendency will be to remember the past relationship as even worse than it was and then to use that inaccurate memory as a guide to what you can expect in the future. The more fearful you become of the future, the more likely you are to exaggerate the pain you felt in the past. The more pain you remember feeling in the past, the more fearful you will be of the future. Your negative emotions feed on themselves, creating both a horrible past and a terrible future.

Remember the study in chapter 4 about anxious people who believed that feeling anxious was a sure sign that they had performed badly in a social situation? Those people are like the students Levine and Safer found, who recalled being more anxious about tests than they really were. These anxious students saw their fear as its own justification: if they felt anxious about a test, that meant not that they had anxious personalities and should calm down, but rather that there was really something to be anxious about and so they should rev up. Feeling anxious, they planned to study more for their final exam than other students who felt less anxious. Yet the more they studied, the more anxious they became. Believing in their fears and trying to defend against them only made them feel more fearful.

Moreover, according to Levine and Safer, people typically overestimate how intense their emotional responses to future events will be, and how long those responses will last. This holds true for both good events (such as the victory of a favorite sports team) and bad ones (such as not receiving tenure). People don't realize how many different factors will affect their feelings after something bad or good happens, how their coping efforts, judgments, and behavior will affect their feelings. Instead, they imagine an intense, long-lasting feeling, whether good or bad, and assume they know it's coming.

What lessons can we draw from these studies? First, be skeptical of how you remember and predict emotion. Remember that you don't know how a certain situation will make you feel. Even if your worst fears come true, you may well overestimate how painful or upsetting the situation will be.

Second, be aware of how unreliable your memories and predictions often are. Just because something feels true doesn't mean it is true. The painful childhood memories of our mother's envy or our father's anger loom large in our minds, and we can't help feeling that they're giving us valuable information about what to expect in the future. But often, the child's-eye view in which Mommy and Daddy seem so big and scary doesn't really tell us much about how we'll actually feel next week, next month, or next year. We feel as though our fears are justified, but they may not be.

Third, when you can, choose a more positive view of the world. Focus on remembering the good rather than the bad, particularly with regard to your own emotions. The more positive memories you have of feeling good, the more confidence and effectiveness you'll carry with you into the future. Feeling confident, effective, and calm creates a positive cycle to replace the vicious one.

Finally, commit to making reality your guide, rather than your emotions. Try to master the difference between "I'm scared of my parents' disapproval" and "My parents' disapproval will destroy me." The first statement is an accurate description of how awful it feels to be afraid. The second is an inaccurate prediction of what is likely to happen. Learning the difference may not make you feel any less frightened, but it may lead you to take more effective actions toward getting the life you really want.

Bringing Reality to Bear on Your Fears

If you would like a bit more practice in bringing reality to bear on your fears, you might return to the exercises "Challenge Your Fear of Fear" on pages 93–95 and "Disengage from Your Anxiety" on pages 102–104 in chapter 4. You also might begin to analyze your fears with the help of the following questionnaire.

QUESTIONNAIRE

Shining the Light of Reality on Your Fears

1. When I think of the goal that means the most to me, the following fears get in my way:

   a. _____

   b. _____

   c. _____

   d. _____

   e. _____

   f. _____

2. The fear that feels most significant from that list is _____
   _____.

3. The worst experience I've ever had with that fear was when
   _____.

4. Here is a detailed description of that experience: _____
   _____.

5. Now that I recall that past experience, here is my prediction of what my future experience is likely to be as I pursue my goal (choose one):

   • Just as bad as that memory

   • Almost as bad as that memory

   • Bad, but not nearly as bad as that memory

- Some-what good

- Very good

You can fill in the questionnaire again, focusing on each of the fears you've identified, and you also can use it again to explore a different goal.

Now that you've discovered your buried dreams, identified your hidden fears, and analyzed how likely it is that your fears will come to pass, let's move on to our final chapter, where you'll decide what matters to you most.

Choose Your Own Path

We live in a culture that values positive thinking, so it's easy to caricature this part of the process. There is a whole world of bumper stickers and refrigerator magnets out there telling you to "Follow your bliss" and promising that "If you dream it, you can do it." As both a therapist and a person, I tend to believe that people can achieve at least some version of their dreams, so I don't want to dismiss the power of such slogans. If they work for you—if they motivate you to pursue the buried dreams you've been neglecting, to push aside your fears, and to pursue your true desires—more power to you.

But, I suspect, if you've chosen to buy this book and if you've read this far in it, following your dreams may not sound so easy to you. Even after you've analyzed your fears and put them into perspective, you may still be wondering how to move forward.

I suppose if I were going to boil down my own advice into a slogan, I'd choose the same words I chose for step 3: Decide what matters most. Look clearly at your fears and then decide what matters most: your concerns about the consequences of your actions, or your vision of the life you want.

I know this isn't necessarily a simple choice. You may decide, for example, that your dreams have too high a price. Perhaps you aren't willing to risk your financial security for a more satisfying lifestyle, or maybe you really do want to put your family's needs ahead of your own. You also may seek some compromises, arrangements in which you accommodate other people or other concerns but still find some way of going for your dreams.

Whatever you decide, my concern is that you make the choice openly and with a full understanding of what you're doing. Many of us think we've made a clear, rational choice, and then we start picking fights with our adviser, or lose focus in our studies; sabotage potentially good relationships or choosing unsuitable partners; develop migraines or other symptoms; the list goes on and on.

So let's take one more look at the signs you may be ignoring in which you're holding yourself back. Return to the checklist in chapter 1 on pages 31–33, "Am I Holding Myself Back without Realizing It?" and to the questionnaire on pages 36–38, "What Do You Want—and What's Holding You Back?" Ask yourself again if there are areas in your life where you've tried to take a certain type of action—and then found ways to sabotage yourself. Revisit as well the questionnaire on pages 43–47 in chapter 2, "Am I Pursuing Goals That I Truly Desire?" Think for a moment about your hidden fears, your buried dreams, and the life you truly want. Then complete the following questionnaire:

QUESTIONNAIRE
What Matters to You Most?

Love/Relationships

1. Suppose you could choose anything you wanted in the sphere of love and relationships. What would you choose? _____
   _____.

2. What part of that do you have now? _____
   _____.

3. What part don't you have now? _____
   _____.

4. What circumstances outside your control are keeping you from getting what you want, and how? _____
   _____.

5. What choices are you making that are keeping you from getting what you want? _____
   _____.

Take a moment to consider what you want and what is preventing you from getting it. Start by visualizing yourself completely happy in the way you imagine would most satisfy you. Then bring into your consciousness the obstacles that stand in your way, both those of your own making and those that come from outside yourself. Then answer the following questions:

6. What, realistically, might you do to overcome those obstacles (whether or not you are willing to do it)? _____
   _____.

7. What future do you envision for yourself if you do not over-come those obstacles? _____
_____.

8. What are you actually willing to do to overcome those obstacles? _____
_____.

Review your answers. Think again about the future you will face based on the choices you are making. Is that the future you want? Have you chosen based on what matters to you most? Take this opportunity to add some final thoughts on the life you want, what matters to you most, and what you're willing to do to get it.

_____
_____.

Work/Career/Vocation

1. Suppose you could choose anything you wanted in the sphere of work, career, and vocation. What would you choose? _____
_____.

2. What part of that do you have now? _____
_____.

3. What part don't you have now? _____
_____.

4. What circumstances outside your control are keeping you from getting what you want, and how? _____
_____.

5. What choices are you making that are keeping you from getting what you want? _____
_____.

Take a moment to consider what you want and what is preventing you from getting it. Start by visualizing yourself completely happy in the way you imagine would most satisfy you. Then bring into your consciousness the obstacles that stand in your way, both those of your own making and those that come from outside yourself. Then answer the following questions:

6. What, realistically, might you do to overcome those obstacles (whether or not you are willing to do it)? _____
_____.

7. What future do you envision for yourself if you do not overcome those obstacles? _____
_____.

8. What are you actually willing to do to overcome those obstacles? _____
_____.

Review your answers. Think again about the future you will face based on the choices you are making. Is that the future you want? Have you chosen based on what matters to you most? Take this opportunity to add some final thoughts on the life you want, what matters to you most, and what you are willing to do to get it.

_____
_____.

Lifestyle/Personal Happiness

1. Suppose you could choose anything you wanted in the sphere of lifestyle and personal happiness (home situation, friendships, leisure time, travel, or any other aspect of your life that is important to you). What would you choose? _____
_____.

2. What part of that do you have now? _____
_____.

3. What part don't you have now? _____
_____.

4. What circumstances outside your control are keeping you
from getting what you want, and how? _____
_____.

5. What choices are you making that are keeping you from
getting what you want? _____
_____.

*Take a moment to consider what you want and what is preventing you
from getting it. Start by visualizing yourself completely happy in the
way you imagine would most satisfy you. Then bring into your consciousness the obstacles that stand in your way, both those of your own
making and those that come from outside yourself. Then answer the
following questions:*

6. What, realistically, might you do to overcome those obstacles
(whether or not you are willing to do it)? _____
_____.

7. What future do you envision for yourself if you do not overcome those obstacles? _____
_____.

8. What are you actually willing to do to overcome those obstacles? _____
_____.

*Review your answers. Think again about the future you will face
based on the choices you are making. Is that the future you want?
Have you chosen based on what matters to you most? Take this opportunity to add some final thoughts on the life you want, what
matters to you most, and what you are willing to do to get it.*

_____
_____.

Reach for a Helping Hand

Throughout this book I've given you lots of support to make better choices. I would love to think that my advice is all you need. But now that you've made it this far, I'll let you in on a little secret: everybody needs help. I don't think I've met a single successful person who didn't have at least one—and usually several—supportive people in his or her corner: a spouse, a friend, a teacher, a colleague, a therapist.

So if you've made some plans to take action toward getting the life you want, more power to you. If you're still struggling with deciding what matters most, be good to yourself and give yourself some time to sort through what may be very challenging choices. Either way, I urge you to surround yourself with helpful, loving people who will support you in your dreams—and possibly also to find a teacher, counselor, therapist, or mentor who can help you see things clearly. Together, you and your support network can move forward to confront your hidden fears, uncover your buried dreams, and create the life you really want.

References

Introduction. The Gorilla in the Room

Freud, Sigmund. "Those Wrecked by Success." In J. Strachey, *Some Character Types Met with in Psychoanalytic Work: The Standard Edition of the Complete Psychological Works of Sigmund Freud, Vol. 14 (1914– 1916): On the History of the Psycho-Analytic Movement: Papers on Metapsychology and Other Works*. New York: W. W. Norton, 1916, 309–333.

Simons, Daniel J., and Christopher F. Chabris. "Gorillas in Our Midst: Sustained Inattentional Blindness for Dynamic Events," *Perception* 28 (1999).

1. Know Your Own Mind—Even if It Scares You

Harvey, Alison G., and Suzanna Payne. "The Management of Unwanted Pre-Sleep Thoughts in Insomnia: Distraction with Imagery versus General Distraction." *Behaviour and Research Therapy* 40 (2002): 267–277.

Jeannerod, M. "Mental Imagery in the Motor Context." *Neuropsychologia* 33, no. 11 (1995): 1419–1432.

Kosslyn, S. M., M. Behrmann, and M. Jeannerod. "The Cognitive Neuroscience of Mental Imagery." *Neuropsychologia* 33 (1995): 1335–1344, citing G. Deutsch, W. T. Bourbon, A. C. Papanicolaou, and H. Eisenberg. "Visuospatial Experiments Compared via Activation of Regional Cerebral Blood Flow." *Neuropsychologia* 26 (1988): 445–452, and A. Richardson, "Mental Practice: A Review and Discussion (Parts I and II)." *Research Quarterly* 38 (1967): 95–107, 263–273.

Wegner, Daniel M. "Ironic Processes of Mental Control." *Psychological Review* 10, no. 1 (1994): 34–52.

2. Imagine the Life That's Right for You

Breznitz, S., ed. *Stress in Israel*. New York: Van Nostrand, 1982.

Clance, Pauline Rose, and Suzanne Imes. "The Imposter Phenomenon in High Achieving Women: Dynamics and Therapeutic Intervention." *Psychotherapy Theory, Research and Practice* 15, no. 3 (Fall 1978): 1–8.

de Vries, Manfred F. R. Kets. "The Dangers of Feeling Like a Fake." *Harvard Business Review* (September 2005): 1–9.

Elliot, A., and T. Thrash. "The Intergenerational Transmission of Fear of Failure." *Personality and Social Psychology Bulletin* 30, no. 8 (2004): 957–971.

Fried-Buchalter, Sharon. "Fear of Success, Fear of Failure, and the Imposter Phenomenon." *Journal of Personality Assessment* 58, no. 2 (1992): 368–379.

Laflamme, L., K. Engstrom, J. Moller, and J. Hallqvist. "Is Perceived Failure in School Performance a Trigger of Physical Injury? A Case-Crossover Study of Children in Stockhold County." *Journal of Epidemiology and Community Health* 58 (2004): 407–411.

Martin, Andrew J., and Herbert W. Marsh. "Fear of Failure: Friend or Foe?" *Australian Psychologist* 38 (March 2003): 1, 31–38.

Nader, Karim. "Memory Traces Unbound." *Trends in Neuroscience* 26, no. 2 (February 2003): 65–72.

Rusch, B., H. Abercrombie, T. Oakes, S. Schaefer, and R. Davidson. "Hippocampal Morphometry in Depressed Patients and Control Subjects: Relations to Anxiety Symptoms." *Biological Psychiatry* 50 (2001): 960–964.

Teevan, R. "Childhood Development of Fear of Failure Motivation: A Replication." *Psychological Reports* 53 (1983): 506.

4. Overcome Your Fear of Fear Itself

Janis, I. L. "Decisionmaking under Stress." In *Handbook of Stress*, 2nd ed. Edited by L. Goldberger and S. Breznitz. New York: Free Press, 1993.

Silverman, M., et al. "Functional Neuroanatomy of Impending Threat: A Novel fMRI Study of Anticipatory Anxiety and Its Healthy Habituation." *Clinical Autonomic Research*.

Wild, Jennifer, et al. "Perception of Arousal in Social Anxiety: Effects of False Feedback during a Social Interaction." *Journal of Behavior Therapy and Experimental Psychiatry* (2007), in press.

5. Free Yourself from Your Fear of Guilt

Darwin, C. "A Biographical Sketch of an Infant." *Mind* 2 (1877): 285–294.

Eisenberger, Naomi, et al. "Does Rejection Hurt? An fMRI Study of Social Exclusion." *Science* 302 (October 10, 2003): 290–292.

————. "An Experimental Study of Shared Sensitivity to Physical Pain and Social Rejection." *Pain* 126 (2006): 132–138.

Hart, Sybil, et al. "Infants Protest Their Mothers' Attending to an Infant-Size Doll." *Social Development* 7, no. 1 (1998): 54–61.

Iyengar, B. K. S. *Light on Yoga: The Bible of Modern Yoga.* New York: Schoken, 1995.

Iyengar, B. K. S., J. Evans, and D. Abrams. *Light on Life: The Yoga Journey to Wholeness, Inner Peace, and Ultimate Freedom.* New York: Rodale Books, 2005.

Panksepp, Jaak. "Feeling the Pain of Social Loss." *Science* 302 (October 10, 2003): 237–239.

Twenge, Jean M., et al. "Social Exclusion Causes Self-Defeating Behavior." *Journal of Personality and Social Psychology* 83, no. 3 (2002): 606–615.

8. Understand Your Fear of Not Being a Real Man or a Real Woman

Backhans, M. C., M. Lundberg, and A. Mansdotter. "Does Increased Gender Equality Lead to a Convergence of Health Outcomes for Men and Women?: A Study of Swedish Municipalities." *Social Science and Medicine* 64, no. 9 (May 2007): 1892–1903.

Balkin, Joseph. "Contribution of Friends of Women's Fear of Success in College." *Psychological Reports* 61 (1987): 39–42.

Barash, Susan Shapiro. *Tripping the Prom Queen: The Truth about Women and Rivalry.* New York: St. Martin's Press, 2005.

Berdahl, Jennifer I. "The Sexual Harassment of Uppity Women." *Journal of Applied Psychology* 92, no. 2 (2007): 425–437.

Heilman, Madeline E., et al. "Penalties for Success: Reactions to Women Who Succeed at Male Gender-Typed Tasks." *Journal of Applied Psychology* 89, no. 3 (2004): 416–427.

Heilman, Madeline E., and Julie J. Chen. "Same Behavior, Different Conse-quences: Reactions to Men's and Women's Altruistic Citizenship Behavior." *Journal of Applied Psychology* 90, no. 3 (2005): 431–441.

Heilman, Madeline E., and Tyler G. Okimoto. "Why Are Women Penalized for Success at Male Tasks?: The Implied Community Deficit." *Journal of Applied Psychology* 92, no. 1 (2007): 81–92.

Horner, Matina. "Toward an Understanding of Achievement-Related Conflicts in Women." *Journal of Social Issues* 28 (1972): 158–175.

Hyland, Michael E., and Anthony V. Mancini. "Fear of Success and Affiliation." *Psychological Reports* 57 (1985): 714.

Leder, Gilah C. "Sex Differences in Attributions of Success and Failure." *Psychological Reports* 54 (1984): 57–58.

Sayer, Liana C., and Suzanne M. Bianchi. "Women's Economic Independence and the Probability of Divorce." *Journal of Family Issues* 21, no. 7 (October 2000): 906–943.

Wilcox, W. Bradford, and Steven L. Nock. "What's Love Got to Do with It?: Equality, Equity, Commitment and Women's Marital Quality." *Social Forces* 84, no. 3 (March 2006): 1321–1345.

10. Get in Touch with Reality

Levine, Linda J., and Martin A. Safer. "Sources of Bias in Memory for Emotions." *Current Directions in Psychological Science* 11, no. 5 (October 2002): 169–173.

Morewedge, Carey K., Daniel T. Gilbert, and Timothy D. Wilson. "The Least Likely of Times: How Remembering the Past Biases Forecasts of the Future." *Psychological Science* 16, no. 8 (2005): 626–630.

Index

adrenaline, 140
aggression, 137, 146–148
anger, 131–133
  aggression *vs.* assertiveness,
    146–148
  awareness of, 133–137
  expression of, 137–139
  hormones and, 139–140, 146
  listening to, 144–145
  overcoming, 141–143
  physical reaction to, 139–140
  positive effects of, 140–141
  self-assessment, 134–137
anxiety, 226
  avoidant behavior and, 61–64,
    89–92
  physical symptoms of,
    93–95
  See also stress
approach/withdrawal behavior,
  116
arrogance
  fear of, 126–129
  fear of envy and, 151

self-confidence *vs.*,
    126–129
assertiveness, 146–148

Balkin, Joseph, 192
Barash, Susan Shapiro,
    191–192
Baumeister, Roy F., 168–170
Berdahl, Jennifer I., 182–183
Beth Israel Deaconness Hospital,
    116
Bianchi, Suzanne M., 193–194
Boston Marathon, 74–75
brain
  anger and, 139–140
  fear and, 95–104
  meditation and, 116
  stress and, 61
  undermining thoughts and,
    20–23
  See also hormones; ironic
    processes of mental control
Breznitz, Shlomo, 60–61,
    101–102